MY LIFE
as a
SPERM

Essays from the Absurd Side

"How appropriate that Gene has chosen to group together a wonderful compendium of his offbeat life events into one easy to read and entertaining volume. Whether he's digging for bones or in pursuit of the Rolling Stones, his bi-coastal adventures are packed with wry observations, and of course, his own unique infectious twists of humor. It was especially enjoyable to relive the chapters from when he was foraging in our area and I'm happy to report they remain as timely and as delightfully 'absurd' as ever."

Barry Fain, Publisher, Providence Media

"We all have stories. But few of us can tell them like Gene Twaronite. In turn, his stories amuse, instruct, entertain, and inspire. You'll smile, chuckle, laugh out loud, wince, and often identify with the life lessons shared in his memories and musings. Best of all, you might decide to turn on the computer and record your own stories. Now that's fine writing!"

Suzanne Barchers, EdD, Advisor and Chair of Board of Directors, Lingokids, Madrid, Spain. Author of 300 books and songs for educators and children

"Gene Twaronite's book is funny and fun, with fascinating scenes of his journey from childhood through a young old age. With wit and honesty, he describes those moments of growing up when we struggle to understand what it all means: the church, our place in the universe, our parents, and teachers. Sometimes whimsical, sometimes hilarious, the stories deftly describe his 1950s neighborhood of unsupervised play outdoors, and no TV at home, his relationship with his dad, dealing with loneliness, and then on to his many jobs, marriage, founding a nature center in New Hampshire, attending a Rolling Stones concert, moving out west, coping with aging. These tales engage the reader in the nostalgia of looking back and remembering those flights of imagination we took in the process of becoming who we are today."

Susan Barlow, Writer and Town Historian, Manchester, CT

Also by Gene Twaronite

The Museum of Unwearable Shoes Poems

Trash Picker on Mars Poems

The Absurd Naturalist: Irreverent Musings on Nature Essays

Approaching Wilderness: Six Stories of Dementia

Dragon Daily News: Stories of Imagination for Children of All Ages

My Vacation in Hell Novel

The Family That Wasn't Novel

GENE TWARONITE

MY LIFE *as a* SPERM

Essays from the Absurd Side

ABSURD LIFE PRESS

My Life as a Sperm

Cover design by Abigail Westbrook, A Source of Joy
Editorial and interior by Kate Robinson, Starstone Lit

Absurd Life Press
ISBN 978-0-578-64085-3
Library of Congress Control Number 2020903161

ACKNOWLEDGMENTS

"How to Choose the Perfect God" first appeared in *Buck Off Magazine.*

"How I Met Vonnegut," "Spawn of Cthulhu," "The Pipe in the Closet," and "Romancing the Stones" first appeared in *East Side Monthly* (Providence, RI).

"Aging Awkwardly," "All in the Family," and "A Painless Guide to Trauma" first appeared in *Wilderness House Literary Review.*

"Lot O. Jobs" first appeared in *Work Literary Magazine.*

CONTENTS

The absurd is the essential concept and the first truth.

—ALBERT CAMUS

But can it dance?

A NOTE TO THE READER

ASIDE FROM THE TITLE ESSAY and "Sex Toys After Fifty," which are absurd flights of my imagination, these essays are largely autobiographical. To the best of my memory, I have related events as they occurred, while occasionally tweaking the narrative, to keep things lively.

I like to think of this as a work of "creative nonfiction," a gloriously elastic category which allows a writer the freedom to explore a subject unfettered by adherence to strict journalistic standards, relating the facts with a certain amount of artistic flair.

As these pieces came together, they took on a life of their own and began to tell a story. In describing a memoir, Gore Vidal wrote that it "is how one remembers one's own life." It is not hung up with precise dates, names and other details of the past, but is more a re-creation of one's life as seen through the author's lens. The emphasis is less on accuracy and more on emotional experience.

When it comes to emotion, tears are overrated. Beware

of anyone who cannot laugh. Run for the nearest exit. In re-creating my life on these pages, I write mostly about events where I can find some humor while eschewing those where, for the life of me, I can't find anything to laugh at. Fortunately for me, these are rare. I like to think that, even on my deathbed, wracked with the pain of knowing not only that my best days are behind me, but that I can no longer remember them, I'll still find plenty of things to crack me up.

Running through each of these essays is a sense of absurdity, for that is the lens through which I choose to see my life and the world.

Though some of these pieces do cuddle up to each other in places, mostly they move back and forth through my life, willy-nilly, like my memories. So, jump in anywhere. The only thing you have to fear is the day you can no longer laugh at yourself.

MY LIFE AS A SPERM

In their ongoing memory wars, memoirists seek to go ever deeper into their pasts, uncovering astonishing details about their first years of life. One writer recalls the intimate conversation she had, at two months old, with her mother and the family priest about whether the soul can enter heaven with heavily soiled diapers, or if God prefers prosciutto or pepperoni pizza.

Not to be outdone, some writers claim to be able to recall their fetal memories as early as thirty weeks after conception. The severely limited social environment of the fetus, coupled with its lack of a comprehensive vocabulary, does pose challenges for the creative writer. Let's face it, there's not a lot of partying going on, and your conversation with the outside world largely consists of kicking. One writer insists, however, that he first decided to become a rock 'n' roll drummer because, while still in the womb, he became habituated to his drunken dad's late-night pounding on the front door.

I must confess that I remember little from my earliest years, aside from bratty episodes when I would scream and cry in the department store to make my poor Aunt Mary buy me a toy elephant, or the way I could put on my "ain't I lovable" act and con my dear grandmother out of another of her stuffed animals. As for my fetus days, forget it–they're a complete blank. But oddly enough, I do possess vivid recollections of my interior life just before conception.

True, there's not enough stuff to fill a book. The whole thing lasted only a few days–just after I entered the womb–but oh what days they were! Looking back now, I have to say it was the most challenging time of my life, full of danger, excitement, and emotional triumphs.

I remember being a lonely guy at the time, despite the fact that I was surrounded by over 250 million of my brothers. I dreamed of finding just the right egg to spend my life with, an egg who would understand me and not make fun of the fact that I was 175,000 times smaller than she was. I was determined to find her.

Up through the deep dark caverns I traveled, with only my raw courage to guide me. It was a perilous journey that few of us would survive. During the first few minutes, I had watched in horror as millions of my band of brothers died in writhing agony in the acid bath of the vaginal canal. Tony and Eddie–such great kidders–

who were always good for a laugh. And who can forget George, who was always tripping on his own tail, or my best bud Frank? Damn, how I miss him! Then came that cervical mucus–like swimming through egg white–where many of the poorer swimmers drowned. So many good men died that day, and for what? The same reason I was there, still alive and swimming toward my dream. I was young and strong and knew that she was up there waiting for me.

My tail ached as I swam and jostled for position. On and on we swam, up through the cervix and uterus, in a grim marathon where only the strongest would survive. At that point, I was swimming on pure DNA. Though few of us who had started the race remained, I knew I could do it. As we got closer to the infamous fallopian tunnels, I could see some poor saps taking the wrong tube. Hate to admit it, but I was not sad to see them go. A few less competitors to get in my way.

Just as I was about to enter the tunnel, I felt her presence for the first time. It was if she were sending me a signal to guide me to her. I started swimming like an Olympic sperm.

Now the real trick in these marathons is to pace yourself. You don't want to burn out too soon, and I still had one big obstacle to overcome.

So, I purposely let some of the other sperm get ahead.

Actually, I had paid them all off beforehand to pass

the torch to me. The idea was for them to arrive at my beloved before I did and start breaking down her resistance with their enzymes. She was very sweet, but had developed a real wall around her.

Suddenly, there she was–the egg of my heart. The guys had done their job, and by the way that she looked at me I knew she felt the same about me. She was ready. In no time, I was in.

For a few blissful days, we traveled together down the fallopian tube. After about a week, the honeymoon was over and it was time to get attached in our new apartment. I wish I could remember more. I'm sure there were some very good times.

GUNS, SPEARS, AND DOLLS

WHILE GROWING UP—still an ongoing process—I don't recall anyone ever telling me how or when to play or whether I was playing too much. My parents encouraged me to read and to get good grades, of course, but I was a nerdy kid who would have done so anyway. Play was just something I did, as natural as breathing or falling on my face.

One time, I played with a shovel and dug for hours in the bare soil behind the shed. As the hole got deeper and my head vanished beneath the surface, I became a paleontologist searching for dinosaur bones. Why not? They could be down there, I thought, waiting for me to discover them. All I had to do was dig. Maybe I would reach the other end of the world. Just imagine—a tunnel through the Earth.

Then I found it. It was a birdlike skull and backbone of some strange creature. It had to be a dinosaur. The fact that it didn't appear to be fossilized and came out of the earth so readily didn't matter. Part of the game, you see, was to believe. For a few minutes, I reveled in the joy of discovery.

Suddenly, a stern voice intruded. "What are you doing?" my dad asked. "And why are you holding that chicken bone?"

Gone was my dream of a new dinosaur or reaching China. Shaking his head, he helped me climb out of the hole. It was not the first time his son had done something stupid. Then he pointed to the hole. "Now get it filled before supper!"

It was a long afternoon. Filling the hole was nowhere near as much fun as digging it. It did teach me a lesson, though. Finding dinosaur bones in your backyard is not that easy.

I remember something else as well. The fact that I had dug a deep and potentially dangerous hole that I could have fallen into didn't seem to bother my dad. He didn't stick around to help or watch over me. You dug it; you fill it.

It does seem that since the 1950s, the period when I at least started to grow up, kids have far less time for unsupervised play, especially outdoors. Increasingly they are protected from dangers, real or imagined, and prodded toward more organized activities or to study harder. They certainly wouldn't be allowed to dig a deep hole in the backyard.

"When does a kid ever get to sit in the yard with a stick anymore?" asked George Carlin. Speaking of sticks, Jonathan Winters was known to improvise with any object handed to him. On the Late Show, Jack Paar once gave Winters a stick and off he went, pretending to be everything from a fisherman to a lion tamer. Which brings me to my own stick adventures.

One day, after my third-grade geography class, I couldn't wait to get home so I could reenact the lesson. It was about a remote native tribe in Brazil, New Guinea, or somewhere, and how they fashioned spears, bows, and arrows out of branches in the jungle to kill the animals they ate or to protect themselves from other tribes. It was a glorious time to be a kid. You didn't run home after school to watch TV. Many families still didn't have one, and both the television sets and program selections were dismal. So, you ended up creating your own entertainment from whatever popped into your head.

I gathered my gang of friends. There were two or three of us boys, accompanied by the minister's daughters who lived across the street. Since it was my idea, I got to set the stage, followed by the inevitable squabbling over who gets to play what. We were already into costume. Shorts and no shirts for boys, shorts and blouses for girls. We fashioned our weapons out of whatever sticks we could find. One girl made a bow, with some featherless arrows that never went anywhere. Most of us simply made spears. I had a readymade one, the shaft of a toy wooden golf club, from which I had removed the head. Sharpening our lethal weapons, we set off into our neighborhood jungle.

After terrorizing some neighbors' dogs and killing scores of imaginary beasts and tribal foes, we were about to set off into the next yard when a towering, fearsome giant appeared, blocking our path. Scared out of our wits, we froze in our tracks. Actually, it was my buddy Mike's dad, who at six foot three did seem like a giant to us. Proud of his physique, he was shirtless as usual. With muscled arms folded across his hairy chest, he glowered with menace.

"What the heck are you guys doing? Do you want to kill someone?" At that point, he grabbed my little golf spear and pointed at its well-sharpened tip. "Look at that. You could put someone's eye out with that." Then he broke it across his knee, and did likewise with the other weapons. Game over.

He had no right to do that, I thought. But I was not about to argue with him. Had to admit, it was not the wisest thing for us to be doing, and he was just redirecting our play into safer channels.

Most of the time, however, there was little playtime supervision. I adored kindergarten. I remember sprawling out on the floor and playing with blocks with my pal Steve, building tall structures perpetually in danger of falling on our heads. Besides the traditional-sized blocks, there were also these polished timbers, sort of like 2 x 6s, with which we made long tunnels snaking across the room. Then we would crawl through them, exploring the dark passages we had made. Our teacher, bless her heart, pretty much left us alone. I can't imagine a kindergarten teacher today ever allowing students to engage in such hazardous construction.

In the same kindergarten room, there was also a full-size dollhouse that you could walk through and play—well, whatever. There were never any boys in there besides me. It wasn't that boys weren't allowed. But I was intrigued. A whole house where you could go inside and play. I can't remember exactly what we played, but I do recall the girls and I had some lovely parties.

It was simple curiosity on my part. I wanted to know what exactly you did in a dollhouse and if it might be fun. It was the same when I briefly took up playing with dolls. I watched girls as they cuddled and cared for their dolls. Could I be missing something? I had to find out.

So, for a while, I had my own baby doll, and loved doing all the nurturing things parents are supposed to do. I never tried breastfeeding, however. There were limits. I still saw myself as a boy trying out something new.

No one ever told me I couldn't, except for my Uncle Johnnie, who took me fishing once and warned me against the dangers of playing with dolls. The fact that none of the other boys in the neighborhood played with dolls didn't bother me. However, my friend Tommy's dad—a real he-man kind of guy—sternly informed me that my dolls and I were no longer welcome in his backyard. Guess he didn't want me infecting his sons.

The interesting thing about this episode is my discovery that there were other kinds of dolls besides infant ones. Once, playing dolls with my two girl cousins, I noticed one of the dolls had a decidedly different look about it. She had a shapely figure, with breasts! She wore high heels and a tight-fitting dress, and underneath it was a bra and girdle. Playing with this doll made me all warm and weird inside. From that day forward, my doll-playing days were over. I had discovered sex.

As a young kid growing up in a strict Catholic family, I could only imagine sex, of course. There was only one kind of play that was forbidden to me, and that was to play with myself. You'd burn in hell if you touched yourself down there. And to play with other kids in that way was unthinkable.

But kids always find a way. They play doctor, for instance. I remember getting my first doctor set at Christmas. My first patients were the minister's daughters across the street. I put on my stethoscope and called the first girl into my office. Her name was Barbara. She was in my class, and every day I walked her home from school. We had a thing for each other, but there was never anything physical. We were too shy to even hold hands. But that day, she did something unexpected. She took off her blouse, baring her naked chest for examination. I took one look and nearly fainted. Then, sputtering an excuse, I grabbed my doctor set and ran home. It took me many years before I could look at a girl's bare chest again.

When not playing dolls or doctor, I played with toy guns. Six-guns, derringers, rifles, shotguns–I loved them all, especially my tommy gun. You pulled back its bolt and it made a high decibel rat-tat-tat that was music to my ears and drove everyone crazy. I'd run from room to room, firing off my gun and mowing down imaginary enemies until some relative would yell, "Get outta here, you're driving me crazy!"

Growing up on Westerns and war movies, guns were always part of my childhood. Later, there were BB and pellet guns, with which I shot starlings and other unfortunate creatures. For a brief time, I even played with real guns, plinking at tin cans in the woods, until I outgrew them.

All through my teens, I loved to take long solitary hikes, imagining myself a mountain man. I would pack a knapsack and strap on a fearsome-looking hunting knife, trekking down my suburban street as if setting off for the wilderness. In those days, while you weren't allowed to walk down the street with a real gun on your hip, no one gave a second thought to a kid packing a Bowie knife in plain view.

Numerous studies have pointed to the importance of play in childhood. Kids will always play, though in new and different ways. In the future, they won't need sticks or toy guns anymore, when they can just touch the screen on a computer and make whatever 3D-printed object they desire. They won't need dolls, when they can act out their fantasies with realistic robots of any age or sex. They won't need an imagination when they can step into a virtual reality holodeck and set the controls for whatever place and time period they wish to visit. It's a good thing those things weren't around when I was growing up. I never would have come out.

Meanwhile, I feel a sudden urge to go out and play, maybe dig a big hole. Too bad I live in an apartment.

THROWING UP CATHOLIC

I WAS RAISED IN A strict Catholic family and took my faith literally, wrestling daily with its extraordinary claims and implications. The way I figured it, what's the point of having a religion if you're not going to take it seriously. Otherwise, it's just a good luck charm or outfit you wear for special occasions.

Maybe this constant angst partially explained why I was always getting carsick as a kid. My dad loved to drive and take us on long trips. Wherever we went—Maine, the Adirondacks, Nova Scotia, Montreal—there I was, in the back seat throwing up. My parents were so worried about me that they finally sent me to the hospital for a series of barium enemas, which is probably why I still glow in the dark whenever I'm having some sort of existential crisis.

Since I attended godless secular schools, I was expected to go to catechism lessons every Saturday morning. There we learned lots of cool stuff about the Trinity (three Gods for the price of one!), the Immaculate Conception (so the

Son of God would not have to go through ordinary channels), Transubstantiation (the belief that the consecration of bread and wine in Communion are transformed into the actual body and blood of Jesus, which had a certain ick factor for me), and the different categories of sin. Right up there among the biggies was denying the existence of God. One nun even tried to convince us that the people who constructed the Titanic were arrogant atheists, going so far as to put "NG" (for "No God") on its bolts. Thus, God had no choice but to cause the ship to hit an iceberg.

But the thing I remember most was how the nuns talked about the soul. Maybe it was just me, but I got the idea that when you're born, the soul is like some clean white sheet out of the washer. But if you aren't careful, it could get stained by sin. Mortal sins–things like heavy petting in the back seat of your car or killing someone–are the worst. They're like spilling black ink all over your soul and as difficult to remove. I couldn't help thinking how badly stained mine must be, and wished I could somehow wash it with bleach and start all over again.

Like most Catholic boys, I spent much of my early years inventing new ways to describe the "m" word in the confessional. My mother kept telling me I was going straight to hell whenever she caught me masturbating. For her, sex was a simple equation: any sex outside marriage, even thinking about it, was a sin. I received no help from my dad, who kept his views largely to himself. (It was only much later that I discovered his extensive collection of *Playboy* in the basement, which he claimed was strictly for investment, like his stamp collection.) Not that I blame him. In my day, dads just weren't into having man-to-man sex talks with their sons. Sometimes, if you were lucky though, they gave you little hints.

One of my most precious memories was when my dad took me as a young kid on a train ride down to New York. I think it was to attend the annual New York Horticultural Society flower show. But first we took a detour to 42nd Street, which at that time had not yet been sanitized and made safe for family viewing, but instead was filled with sex shops of every imaginable kind. I remember how we strolled past the shops, and I looked up at my dad's face gazing through the windows with an expression I had never seen before. Then I too looked at the various objects and pictures on display and was filled with a sense of fear and wonder. In his own clumsy way, I guess, he was trying to tell me something about sexuality, though I had no clue what it was. Neither of us said a word as we headed to the flower show.

The trick about confession is you had to choose the right priest. There were a couple of young priests at my church who were pretty hip. You would watch to see which confessional they entered, or try to hear the sound of their voices inside. Since none of my sins were heavy-duty kinds like adultery or armed robbery and, in fact, 99 percent could be generally classified under the heading of "having impure thoughts," you generally got off easy with those guys. Sometimes I could swear I heard them chuckling softly to themselves when I told them how many times I had abused myself in this manner. Most times, I got off with a couple of Hail Marys and a promise to think about other things besides sex, which at my age was not easy.

But woe to you if you got one of the older priests, far removed from the passions of teen years. One of them had a voice so loud that everyone in the church could hear when he yelled at me, as if I had committed rape, murder, or stealing from the Sunday collection box. I would be lectured on the blackness of my soul and the fires of hell that awaited those with impure thoughts. Then for penance, I would have to do the Stations of the Cross on my knees backward, say the rosary a hundred times, and pray to Holy Mary, Mother of God, every day for a month to deliver me from evil.

High school dating became a constant battleground between God and the evil lust stirring within me. I would make out on the couch with my girlfriend, trying to savor the passion while tormented by my sin. It wasn't until later that I fully realized how much this warped view of sexuality had stunted my emotional growth as a child and teenager, delaying my appreciation of a fuller, richer view of human sexuality, which I still hope to achieve someday.

While battling lust, I was also searching for meaning. At one point, I seriously contemplated a religious vocation, based on my own personal version of Pascal's Wager. Blaise Pascal was a seventeenth-century French philosopher who argued that a smart person should bet God exists and thus believe in Him, since if God does not exist, all you've lost is finite (all the fun you might have had), but if God *does* exist you could stand to lose an infinite gain (eternal heavenly bliss and all that), and have to face an infinite loss (eternal hell fire). It sounded to me as if the smart money was on God. If the God of my Catholic faith really existed, then to risk an eternity in heaven for the brief pleasures of a mortal life would be folly. Why not go for the sure thing? I considered becoming a Franciscan brother. The idea of a simple spiritual life fully given to God was one I devoutly wished to believe in—I also liked the robe and sandals. It would make choosing what to do with my life so much easier.

In my teen years, I tried to be as religious as I could, though I drew the line at self-flagellation and starving myself in the desert. I attended mass daily, and spent long hours meditating before the altar while pretending to have visions of God. What I finally learned from this is that if you think hard enough about seeing something, you'll eventually see it. You get this thing forming in your head and you say, of course, that's God, when all you've seen is your own imagination at work. I imagined God as this pure white light–OK, not very original–which I could hold in my mind for only a microsecond before thoughts intruded. Some people claim to hear God as well, but try as I might I could never pull that off, though one time I heard a buzzing sound which got louder and louder but just turned out to be cicadas. I read books about the saints and set up a small desk as a shrine in my bedroom, where I lit votive candles and prayed daily. Which is why I still love the sight and smell of burning candles tinged with old oak.

One thing about Catholicism, it really focuses the mind on the nature of evil, so much so that when I had to choose a book for a book report in fifth grade, I chose the *Inferno* by Dante Alighieri. Like any kid, I was immediately attracted by the book's subject: a journey through hell. Cool. You'll notice I didn't pick Paradiso (Paradise), Dante's third installment of *The Divine Comedy*. For me, eternal happiness, with all its angels and blissful souls, didn't have quite the same fascination as eternal damnation.

I quickly discovered, however, that the book was written by a guy in the early fourteenth century. As you might imagine, the book was tough slogging, especially for a fifth grader. The worst part was, the author wrote the whole thing as one long poem which starts off like this:

Midway in our life's journey, I went astray from the straight road and woke to find myself alone in a dark wood . . .

Talk about your dark wood. The only thing that got me through it was that in my edition of the book, translated from the Italian by John Ciardi, there was a summary of each canto or chapter, sort of like *Cliff's Notes.* You could just read the summary and then go straight to the good parts. My teacher, by the way, really believed that I read the whole thing and gave me an "A" for "choosing such a mature and complex book."

And, despite having to skim over all the stuff about goodness and virtue and the different categories of sins, I found there were lots of fun parts. I mean, this guy wrote about hell as if it really existed. And he filled it with the souls of people in real heavy-duty pain.

In the third circle, for instance, he described how a storm of stinking freezing rain falls forever on the souls of gluttons, who must sit in a pool of putrid slimy slush, which they are forced to eat while being ripped and torn apart by Cerberus, the official three-headed dog of hell. Is that great or what?

But as I thought about it, doubts began to emerge. For instance, I couldn't see why Dante chose such a terrible punishment for the gluttons of this world. All right, so it's not exactly cool to spend every minute stuffing your face, but does a person really deserve to sit in putrid waste for all time simply because of an eating disorder?

There were other things in the book that I didn't agree with. For instance, in the first circle of hell, Dante puts all the people who never heard about Jesus Christ and thus never had the chance to believe that he was truly God. He calls them the "Virtuous Pagans." Though they don't actually suffer, they have no hope at all. To me this doesn't sound fair. Nor very Christian. Even back then, I knew that there were many other religions in the world, full of people who fervently believed in their own version of God, devoid of Christ. And to have no hope at all forever–well, wouldn't that be the very worst kind of suffering?

My mother always insisted that it's important for a person to believe in something. But just because a person doesn't, does that mean he deserves to go to hell? Aren't there far worse things that people do?

This set off a train of thought that I still engage in, to this day. I highly recommend it as a fun activity to keep things lively at dull parties. For example, what is the absolutely worst thing that a person could do? I guess killing another human being is pretty bad, but it's how you do it that counts. If you kill someone by accident or because you're so mad that you can't think straight, that's one thing. But if you kill someone simply because you're bored or because it brings you pleasure, that's a different story. And if you kill thousands of people because of racial or ethnic hatred or just to make a quick profit or be rewarded in heaven, yes, I think that's got to be right up there on the "worst things" list.

Just read any history book and you'll discover all kinds of nasty things that people have done to each other. There's rape, torture, and cannibalism. There's gassing, goring, and burning at the stake. Or how about the Rwandan Genocide, in which up to a million people or more were killed in a hundred days? Butchered not by armies or bombs, but by neighbors with machetes. Then there's Japanese Lieutenant-General Ishii Shiro and his army of gruesome researchers who, from 1937-1945, conducted lethal experiments on Chinese and Russian prisoners, vivisecting them, often without anesthesia; injecting them with diseases such as syphilis, anthrax, and gonorrhea, raping women to study their fetuses, and even burning people alive. And all for what? To make Japan a world power.

Even with all this evil in the world, I found myself wondering if there were still something worse, something so terrible that we just can't imagine anyone ever doing it. And if someone did do such a thing, how would this person be punished? How much pain and suffering would be enough? Pretty depressing stuff, but I just couldn't help myself. It was fun thinking about it, just as Dante must have felt. He put all kinds of people down in his hell, including famous warriors, philosophers, politicians, and even popes. Speaking of popes, how about all those popes and bishops who during their watch turned a blind eye to priests who sexually abused young boys and girls? Though I no longer believe in hell, I must admit there are days when I still miss it. Maybe we could bring it back, just for special occasions.

In college, I continued my search for answers, taking courses in philosophy and comparative religion, and going on retreat with a Franciscan friend. After much study and reflection, I found all the arguments used to support Catholicism totally unconvincing. The sheer number of other possible beliefs, in fact, made me begin to wonder how to know which was true or false. How can we say that one is better or worse than the others? To say that mine is the one true religion or that my God is better than your God sounds so childish.

But in the end, I kept replaying that question I had first asked myself: Does the God of my Catholic faith really exist? To truly answer it required that I look deep within myself to a place most of us would rather not go, that dark hole of doubt at the center of our being that forever gnaws at whatever certainty we might possess. I was forced to admit that there was at least the possibility that God did not exist, despite all claims to the contrary. I remember the first time I had this thought it struck me with a blinding flash, like a reverse St. Paul on the road to Damascus. Once I admitted even the slightest possibility of God's nonexistence, the elaborate scaffolding I'd so painstakingly constructed to keep my faith secure began to crumble.

I've been a science nerd since childhood, and gradually the more skeptical, critical side of me began to assert itself. I began to see the God question in terms of evidence, or lack thereof. The so-called "proofs" of God's existence I had studied in college were arguments based on faulty logic, not scientific evidence.

Some of the silliest proofs were the various ontological arguments. Anselm of Canterbury, for instance, defined God as "that than which nothing greater can be thought." From there he made the huge jump that if something exists in the mind, then it must also exist in reality. So, in effect, you could just bring something into being by simply thinking about it. Ah, the power of magical thinking. Wouldn't it be nice?

Both Aristotle and Aquinas famously made the cosmological argument that everything that comes into being must have a cause, and therefore the universe must have a first cause we call God. They both insisted that there can't be an infinite series of causes without providing a good reason why. But why not? If God created the universe, then where did God come from? Like the World-bearing Turtle of various Hindu, Chinese, and Native American myths, is it Gods all the way down?

Why not a universe that has always been here? Or a universe forever popping in and out of existence? Indeed, according to modern science, there could be multiple universes. Perhaps the universe is all that is and all that ever will be. Just because our limited minds can't conceive of such a thing, why assume that the universe had to be created? Personally, I find this universe compelling and complete enough, without additional explanation or justification. When I look up at the night sky, with its billions of galaxies, or consider the complexity of life, including my own, I am filled with awe and wonder. I glory in this amazing universe, awaiting our discoveries, while fully accepting that there are mysteries we may never know.

I think the fact that, from an early age, I was scientifically literate helped me come to examine my religion with a more detached and critical perspective. I came to realize that all the great advances made by our species have come not through religion, but through science and its specific method of inquiry based on measurable evidence subject to rigorously defined rules and steps. If it weren't for science, we would still be trembling in the dark calling up various deities whenever it thundered or the sun appeared to go away. And people would still believe diseases were caused by evil spirits and be burned at the stake for witchcraft or for claiming the earth revolved around the sun.

The late astronomer and writer Carl Sagan helped to popularize the much-cited quote: "Extraordinary claims require extraordinary evidence." That God exists is an extraordinary claim, one that can neither be proved nor disproved by science. In terms of real proof–observable, testable knowledge based on demonstrable and reproducible data–there is none. In the end, there is no rational reason to believe in God. I must accept it on faith. But why would a God create us in His own likeness only to insist that we must ignore our highest faculty, the power of reason? My only choice is to renounce my rational side–the part of me I most value–and take a leap of faith into darkness. And, after a deliberate and personally painful process, I finally realized that, for me, it was a leap too far.

I think many of us are reluctant to put our faith under the microscope and examine it closely. What if Pascal was right? Better be safe and keep some faith in your pocket, just in case. Better to not face the possibility that you could be wrong. But what good is a religion that is never questioned or put to the test?

Having gone through this struggle, I think I better understand not only myself, but the powerful appeal that religion still holds for many people. And I try to stay calm and smile when some self-assured true believer presumes to tell me the good news of God's Kingdom to come.

Best of all, I no longer get carsick.

IMAGINING WILDERNESS

WHILE SITTING ON A ROCK overlooking the Lamar Valley in Yellowstone National Park, I gazed beyond the grass and sage-covered plains to a more distant view. In my mind's eye, I followed the Lamar River drainage, exploring lonely dark spruce-fir forests and meadows in the footsteps of grizzlies and wolves. An hour earlier, on a park road jammed with tourists, I had actually seen my first wolves—a few specks of black dancing at the edge of my vision. And I imagined what it would be like to wind among sagebrush that had known the touch of wolves.

It is a trip that I have taken many times since. With each passing year, its memories grow more vivid and no less meaningful to me than if I had actually backpacked into that wilderness.

In this case, there was at least some link to actuality. I was in my sixties and at last had fulfilled my dream of visiting this iconic national park. The wilderness lay just ahead, not far from where I sat. I could almost smell the sagebrush on the wind. All I had to do was head for the horizon and keep walking. But why bother, when I had already imagined it.

Lately, I have visited other wilderness areas as well, with no sensory link other than a book, map, or video image. When I look at these areas on a map, running my fingers over the contour lines, I feel a connection in a real sense. I have stood at the very Gates of the Arctic, surrounded by virtual black flies, flower-covered tundra, and the immense solitude of the Brooks Range. I have wandered through alpine meadows of the John Muir Trail from Yosemite all the way to Mount Whitney and explored the endless hidden canyons of Escalante. And I have visited, at no expense, the fabled islands of Galapagos, where I have marveled at giant tortoises and marine dragons and followed the path of Darwin.

Being a dreamer, it's a wonder I didn't think of this sooner. It might have saved me a lot of grief and confusion.

Growing up, I was always a bookish loner. Since my earliest childhood, I have imagined wilderness, chiefly from the books I read. Writers such as John Muir, Sigurd F. Olson, William O. Douglas, and Edward Abbey provided such glowing firsthand accounts of wild places that I could feel myself there beside them. With Sigurd Olson I have skated down a silvery mirrored lake in the Quetico-Superior country, bathing in an aurora's shimmering light. I have swayed in the treetops with John Muir as he described it in

"A Wind-Storm in the Forests." Once, while out walking in gale-force winds through a New Hampshire forest, I considered recreating Muir's experience by climbing a tall white pine. The feeling lasted only a moment, then was quickly suppressed by common sense.

Indeed, we are indebted to writers such as these for instilling a love and thirst for wilderness that provided the first impetus for its preservation. Together with paintings and photographs, these earliest accounts of Grand Canyon, Yellowstone, Yosemite and other scenic wonders first stirred the imaginations of urban readers, often far removed from these places, to support legislation to preserve them. Only later would some have the chance to visit these places. But first we had to imagine them.

Starting in my teens, I would take long walks alone through the tame parks and state forests of Connecticut suburbia. Though a far cry from real wilderness, they provided me with a stage to act out the fantasy that I was some kind of wilderness superman, aloof from the world, sufficient unto myself, sustained only by my love for wildness. So powerful was the image that by high school I had convinced myself that the only path for me was to become a natural resource professional, protecting wildlife, forests, and scenery in the great outdoors.

I think my dad had something to do with this. He was always telling me about how he wanted to be a forest ranger. His parents couldn't afford to send him to college, however, and he eventually landed a job as a postman with the U.S. Postal Service. There he remained and raised a family, in the small suburban city where both he and son were born. He seemed to be content with the life he had made, and I wonder if he would have been as happy spotting forest fires or cruising timber in some remote corner of the wilderness.

Rebellious child of the sixties, I was going to be different, not chained down by the stultifying sameness of Connecticut suburbia. Like my dad, I was a dreamer, but I was about to be kicked in the head.

In hindsight, I should have seen it coming, but I was a cocky, know-it-all kid who thought he had life all figured out. There were plenty of clues, if I had ever bothered to look. My dad, for instance, for all his talk of being a forest ranger, was a real homebody, a man who didn't stray far from his front door. In so many ways, I was just like him. Yes, we took hikes in the woods, but not once did he ever suggest we try roughing it. Family trips to the Adirondacks and White Mountains always involved a well-stocked ice chest and clean, comfortable hotels. All I remember from the few times I tried backpacking myself was how much *fun* it is carrying forty pounds on your back, how hard it is to sleep with tree roots and rocks projecting into your butt, and the sinister rustling sounds that a mouse can make outside your tent.

Unlike my dad, affording college was no obstacle. So in 1967, at the end of my freshman year as a major in wildlife management at the University of Connecticut, I was ready to test myself against the wilderness. One of my professors had landed me an entry-level federal job for the summer cruising timber for the U.S. Forest Service, in the remote town of Cougar, Washington. Yes, that was its actual name. It sounded every bit as wild as my dreams. For weeks before I left, I lorded it over my friends. I was off to the wilderness–a real mountain man. Even bought my first sleeping bag.

The big day came, and my parents saw me off on my first airline trip–a red eye flight–to Portland, Oregon. There, early the next morning, I was picked up by a kindly Forest Service employee who drove us fifty miles northeast into Washington and the rugged mountains of the southern Cascades in Gifford Pinchot Natural Forest. Raised in New England, I had never seen such wild country in my life. Glacial rivers surging through ravines of giant boulders. Trees hundreds of feet tall, with trunks so massive it would take six men to span them. Forests that seem to go on forever. I was both giddy and slightly frightened. This was no imagined wilderness.

We finally reached camp where I was handed my first big dose of reality. The deal I had signed on for had stated that the Forest Service would provide lodging with a bed and a shared room. The supervisor informed me, however, that all the rooms were filled. He assigned me to a cot in a huge tent shared by a few dozen fellow employees, all of whom snored so loud it's a wonder the tent didn't come down. Inside the tent, it was hot by day and freezing cold by midnight, and despite my sleeping bag I shivered most of the night. Nobody had told me I would spend the summer camping.

My first two days on the job involved cruising timber with a professional forester. I took turns with another new guy measuring and recording such things as tree species, diameter at breast height (DBH), height, and defects. After a while, I got the hang of it, though the forester became increasingly frustrated with me at how all the number 2's that I recorded in the entry book always looked like "S." I could tell it was really starting to bug him. To this day, I can't write the numeral two without wondering if it looks like an "S."

On Saturday morning, a bunch of us temps went out on a hike along a nearby river. There were elk tracks winding everywhere through the giant, moss-covered trees. We approached one huge Douglas fir, and it took six of us to get our arms around its circumference. And there in the distance was the snow-covered summit of Mount St. Helens. Little did I know that in thirteen years it would blow its top and lay waste to much of this forest.

That evening, we went into the local town and headed for the bar. I wasn't into drinking back then, but I enjoyed shooting some pool and swapping stories. I remember one guy in particular, who made quite an impression on me. Frankly, he scared me. He had grown up in Washington and loved the back country more than anything else. He wanted to get as far back in the timber as he could to get away from people and modern civilization. "All you folks coming here from back East," he said, his eyes ablaze with righteousness, "are ruining this state. Soon there won't be any wilderness left." For him, the state was already too crowded. People were the problem, and as far as he was concerned, they could all go to hell. Who needed 'em?

It's funny how one conversation can bring everything into sudden focus. Up until that moment, I had thought that maybe things would be fine and that I could tough it out. Sure, I was homesick and had to sleep in a damn tent. Deal with it. But suddenly all the thoughts and impressions of the past few days crashed head on with my romantic notions of wilderness and myself. Is this really the life I wanted, a life alone in the wilderness? All I really knew was that I was not that guy back in the bar. I could hear Barbara Streisand singing "people who need people" in my head. It was all a mistake and I had to get out of there fast.

My supervisor tried to talk me out of it, then shook his head and accepted my abrupt resignation. He had seen it all before. Everyone was remarkably cool about it. The forester who had driven me into camp agreed to take me back to Portland and even loaned me the money to catch a flight back East. I came home with tail dragging between my legs, and started life over again. The worst part was the way my dad looked at me as he saw his dream to be a forest ranger go up in smoke again.

Of course, I still dream of what my life might have been if I had stuck it out, a life full of adventures in the wilderness. But it wasn't me. And as I look back on the life I made for myself, I wouldn't trade it for all the adventures in the world. Yes, it was painful and embarrassing to come home and admit my mistake. But if I hadn't made that journey, I would never have found out who I really am.

I still dream of wilderness, and even hike there sometimes. Though I'm certainly no John Muir or Bob Marshall, I have logged enough wilderness hours to know some of the sensory images and feelings that only such places can provide. Each of my wilderness hikes, even if only for a few hours, has been a privileged moment. Whether in one of the great wilderness parks like Death Valley, Canyonlands, or Yellowstone, or in some smaller corner of wildness in Maine, New Hampshire, or the Great Smokies, I experience the same kind of emotion. I become a different person. Crossing the wilderness boundary, I can feel myself expanding, filling with new possibilities. These moments have provided me with a sensory record of detailed memories that I can call up faster than a mouse click. With this record I can not only recreate these actual trips but, by using input from many sources, including words and images of wilderness recorded for me by others, build upon them to create entirely new trips in my mind.

There are definite advantages to this kind of trip. Age, physical ability, and money are no obstacles. There are no bugs, rapids, or grizzlies. Also, if we agree that wilderness areas are precious, does it then follow that *all* of us must visit them? I doubt that the American wilderness would long survive such a loving assault. Maybe it's better that most of us limit ourselves to an occasional visit, making do for the most part with experiences of the virtual kind–the kind that leave no footprints.

This is not about turning wilderness into some kind of video game. For no matter how convincing the experience might seem, there is no substitute for the actual. It is the source of all images, all input. The virtual wilderness is only as good as its programming, and for that we need raw data from the real thing to feed into our devices and dreams.

I suspect imagining wilderness will become easier in the near future, with virtual reality helmets and "interactive imaging systems." Fascinated as many of us are with technology, I can imagine a time when virtual wilderness trips become so vivid and convincing that people may prefer them to the real thing. After all, why get wet when you can just put on a helmet and float down the Colorado? Who am I to judge when I can still get a virtual thrill from reading about John Muir swaying in the wind atop a tree?

I now live in Tucson, a city surrounded by mountains and bona fide Sonoran Desert wilderness. On a recent short hike at Sabino Canyon, I paused to rest my stiff, arthritic limbs. Just ahead was a sign marking the wilderness boundary. I gazed up longingly at the steep trail winding for miles through the solitary feeder canyons, where new wonders beckon . . . if only my feet would take me there. But a man can always dream.

HOW I LOST MISS MAINE

FOR THE RECORD, I NEVER really *had* Miss Maine. As relationships go, I actually spent only a short time with her. But for a brief glorious few weeks, she liked me and I liked her. Did I mention she had been a Miss America contestant?

I'm not going to describe her. I can't even remember her name. In a word, she was gorgeous, the kind of woman you can't help but ogle as she walks across the room. But she was also personable and intelligent, not at all like the doe-eyed, dumb stereotype of beauty contestants.

Late in my senior year at college, I was grabbing some lunch in the cafeteria when a female friend came up to me and whispered in my ear, "She's new in our dorm," pointing at Miss Maine, who for the purpose of this narrative, I've decided to call Doris. "She noticed you and wants to be introduced." Apparently, I was not looking my usual wasted self. I shot a glance across the cafeteria and tried to look cool.

As I recall, we had a couple of dates and that was it. I graduated shortly thereafter and landed a residential teaching job at a private school in Connecticut. In addition to my teaching duties, I had a dorm full of teenage boys to look after. There was a big dinner and dance for all the students, and since faculty members were expected to attend, I decided to give Doris a call and see if she wanted to go. Amazingly enough, she said yes.

I picked her up at my alma mater, where she was now a senior, and brought her back to my school. It was early, so we went up to my room in the boys' dormitory and had a couple of stiff drinks before dinner. During my senior year, I had taken up drinking in a big way, but now it was a full-blown avocation, especially during awkward social events as this night was turning out to be. A couple of times during the dance, we snuck back to my room for some more refreshments. I did not notice or care that she was not matching my intake.

What happened after the dance remains hazy. Suddenly we were back in my room, where after refusing my offer of a nightcap, she informed me in no uncertain terms that I was too shit-faced to drive her back to campus. Like a drill sergeant, she instructed me to climb into bed. Then she turned off the light and undressed, donning one of my shirts as a nightie. My kind of woman, I thought to myself. Just like that, I had achieved the goal I had long desired.

Alas, my night of passion was not to be. As I tried to snuggle up and put on my best night moves, she pushed me away with surprising strength. "You're going to sleep it off for a couple of hours," Doris insisted. There in the darkness, I dimly perceived the absurdity of my situation. Here I was–a lusty twenty-two-year-old lying next to a beautiful woman, and I was powerless to do anything about it. After making one last futile pass, I gave in to sleep. A few hours later, I was sober enough to drive her home in silence.

And what did I learn from this lesson? Nothing. I was still twenty-two and stupid. I confess there were many more such events in my life, though none so poignant as that dark, unfulfilled night.

Fortunately, I am here to report that no one died as a result of my wasted youth, including me.

These days, though I still enjoy kicking back with a couple of glasses of wine after dinner, gone is my need to get hammered. Sometimes I catch myself looking back fondly on those old recreational drinking days, while at the same time wincing at the physical and emotional agonies they brought. I think of all the people done in by drinking and driving, and I am quietly thankful. There, partly out of sheer dumb luck but mostly for the grace and good sense of fellow travelers, go I. Thank you, Doris, wherever you are.

NATIVE EARTHLING

I WAS A NATIVE, ONCE. It was back in 1980 when I still lived in my home city of Manchester, Connecticut, and all the time before that from the moment of my birth. But on the day in June when I moved elsewhere, I could no longer call myself a native. Automatically I became a newcomer, outsider, alien—doomed to spend the rest of my life staring blankly at "NATIVE" license plates and bumper stickers.

You only get one shot at being a native. Move away from your birthplace for any substantial amount of time and you are no longer one of the chosen. It matters not if you live in a new place for fifty years, even for the rest of your life. The only way to reclaim your inheritance is to go back home and say you made a mistake. And if your town is now underwater—drowned by a dam for the good that is always presumed greater—you are out of luck.

Natives often speak of their heritage with a sense of accomplishment, as if they had something to do with it. *I was born here*, says the native. *I chose to remain . . . while you did not.*

Well, pardon me for living, but just because you accidentally happened to be born in Scarsdale, London, or on the Mayflower doesn't make you any better than someone born in Somalia, Bangladesh, or Haiti. Staying put is easy, especially if your native home isn't currently being blown to smithereens or sinking below the waves of rising seas. Sometimes you don't have a choice.

I don't care how royal, pure, or blue your blood is, or how your ancestors first cleared this land of native "savages" to make way for civilized white folks, at some point your genetic line had to come from somewhere else. This is what our species has always done, spreading outward from our evolutionary and cultural cradles to occupy all inhabitable spaces on the planet. We humans are always on the move.

There is danger, however, in too much movement. People who do not (or cannot due to forces beyond their control) remain in one place for a time miss out on one of life's grand experiences—a sense of being part of a place, of sharing in its daily rhythms, of knowing that home is much more than comfortable surroundings.

Where does that leave me, a non-native son who has squandered his inheritance? I could try to go back to the life of my late father, a true native of our home city. Ironically, he had to briefly relinquish his claim during his last few years at an out-of-state assisted living center, though his remains have now returned to their ancestral soil. By choosing to stay there all his life, he knew and felt things about that "City of Village Charm" that I will never know.

But there are also many things that my father never got the chance to experience. The world beckons with possibilities. While some of us choose to be natives of one place, others like me cannot help but see each place as merely one aspect or extension of a larger home. Though I may dwell in and derive meaning from a particular location for a time, it can never be my full address. I am of this world as well as in it, a fact more real to me than the temporary happenstance of where I reside. My love for this native home transcends the love I feel for any one place, region or country. I get a lump in my throat whenever I see its portrait in space–a blue-white haven of hope amidst the black emptiness of space–planet number three, home. Home to life. Home to mountains, deserts and seas, great empty spaces and great crowded spaces. Home to more wonderful things, creatures, and peoples than I will ever know.

I think I will stay here awhile. After all, I was born and raised here. No extraterrestrial am I. Call me a native Earthling.

LOT O. JOBS

EVEN WHEN YOU'RE WRITING about something you think is completely different, in the end you're always writing about yourself. Each of us has a unique take on life, and elements of this will invariably creep into your work, no matter how rigorously objective you try to be. In my middle grade fantasy novel, *The Family That Wasn't*, for instance, I created a character with the pen name Lot O. Jobs. He was the author of an autobiography, *Travels of a Mixed-Up Man*, in which he described the hundreds of different jobs he had held, each with its own special flavor. The character didn't just pop out of my head. He's me, of course.

Not that I've had hundreds of jobs. Let's just say I've had my share. And yes, I'm still mixed-up.

I remember my first job as paperboy for the *Hartford Courant*, in Connecticut, supposedly the oldest continually published newspaper in the United States. I should explain here, particularly for younger readers, that a newspaper is a multi-paged object composed of wood pulp, filled with news of local and world events, that is published daily or weekly and requires you to hold it up at arm's length to read while you flip through the pages and grimace before using them to line your parakeet's cage.

Since it is a morning paper, I was required to rise at 5 a.m., which for a school kid, is inhumane. Fortunately, my dad, being a mailman, was used to getting up early. He would wake me, then put on some strong coffee. I forced myself to drink it because it was the only way to stay awake and get moving.

Then I had to walk two blocks to where a half dozen bundles of newspapers awaited me. In those days, if you took on a newspaper route you didn't get to cancel delivery on account of weather. Just like my dad's mail, newspapers were to be delivered through rain, snow, sleet, flood, hurricane, earthquake, volcano, or nuclear war, the latter being very much a possibility in my early youth. So if we had a big snowstorm, and all the schools had snow days, you were still expected to trudge through two feet of snow and deliver your damn papers. Often it would take me hours to finish delivering my route, while my buddies were out sledding.

Delivery was bad enough, but then came the hard part—collecting each week from my cruel, miserly customers. This was before the days of credit card subscriptions. Each Friday evening—and the following Saturday morning if that didn't work–I was expected to ring doorbells and politely ask people to pay up. You wouldn't believe the lengths some people will take to avoid paying what they owe. They would simply hide and not answer the doorbell. In some cases, I could plainly see them scurrying around inside like trapped roaches. Other times, they would let out their big ugly dogs in the yard, timed just before I showed up. Or they would purposely avoid being home, for weeks on end, then when I did finally catch them home would question my accounting and try to convince me that they couldn't possibly owe for two months. I did have my little pay stubs to prove otherwise, but they would then accuse me of forgetting to hand them out when they had obviously already paid. And forget getting any tips. How dare I accuse them of not paying? I suspect many of them secretly enjoyed this game of screwing the paperboy. I think this is when I first became deeply cynical about human nature.

During high school, I was a page at our local library, a dream come true for a bookworm like me, though the wages sucked. The job involved mostly re-shelving returned books. I simply wheeled my cart of books through the aisles where, for a brief time, I diligently placed the books in their proper locations. After a short time, however, I learned how to find a quiet, secluded section of the stacks, preferably upstairs and out of sight of the main desk. This was where the benefits came in. As long as I stood in front of my still full cart, I could make it look as if I were working while reading to my heart's content. That is, until the hatchet lady head librarian invariably found me, chewing me out so badly I didn't dare do it again until next day.

I think back on her fondly and can still see the poor woman chasing us pages through the stacks, shaking her long, bony finger in stern chastisement.

There was one other aspect of the job I should mention. It involved taking reference room calls to retrieve past issues of magazines and newspapers from the basement, where such materials were stored. I would be issued slips of paper, with names of the items and dates published. In those ancient days, you couldn't simply Google something on your smartphone or computer and find a hundred online articles on the subject. There were no personal computers and no digital information. Repeat, no digital information. Let that sink in for a moment. Any information you needed could be found only on the printed page. So there I was, lifting up piles of musty magazines, searching for some obscure issue, only to discover that it had been lost or misplaced. It was sort of like the great lost Library of Alexandria, where all the world's knowledge at the time was stored on scrolls. Being a page back then was probably a lot harder.

In my senior year of college, I briefly had the best job a lonely, testosterone-fueled young male could ask for. It was only part-time, in the evening, but the benefits were priceless. I was the designated male host–sort of a bodyguard–in a women's residence hall. All I had to do was sit behind a front desk and check male visitors in and then escort each of them off the premises at a set time, defined by each dorm. A word of explanation here. I went to college during the late 1960s when many colleges and universities had what were referred to as parietal hours, limited times when men were allowed to visit and mingle with women in the female dormitories. Dorms would often insist that doors be kept open and couples instructed to keep "three feet on the floor." Talk about thwarting your sex life.

Of course, creative women would always find ways around restrictions to get their men inside. Meanwhile, as I sat at the desk–studying, of course–young ladies wearing slinky nightgowns or pajamas would come downstairs and greet me, offering cookies and snacks. I was treated like a god. Even the kindly old dorm matron liked me. I admit, it was quite possible that some diversionary tactic was in play here, with dozens of guys sneaking past me as the women plied me with cookies. But what did I care? Life was good.

My other part-time job in college was as freshman counselor during my senior year. In exchange for a free room in my dormitory, I was expected to offer information and advice to incoming freshman. You can imagine what a perfect fit this was, wise old senior enjoying my own first year on campus after commuting three years. In the midst of cramming as much drinking and carousing with women as humanly possible into just two semesters, I did manage to fit in some actual counseling. Not that I had much advice to offer. Mostly I just listened. And sometimes I would break up unruly dorm parties at 2 a.m., for which at the end of the year I was ceremoniously awarded a carved wooden wand in the shape of a penis with the words "King Prick," signed by my grateful freshmen.

Fresh out of college, and not finding any suitable positions based on my considerable experience drinking and guarding co-eds, I took a job as science teacher at a small residential private school for emotionally disturbed kids. As part of my forestry major, I had taken some basic science courses, and that was good enough. The fact that I had no educational certification or training, and even more important, no psychological or counselor training, did not matter in the least. I was a warm body who knew how to dress for an interview and to give the right answers. And they were desperate for someone who knew at least a little about science and would be willing to work for slave wages.

My first experience with one of my new charges gave me a clue of the challenges ahead. As part of my duties, I sat behind a desk after class in the administration building, as a faculty member on call to assist students with their homework. One of my female students—an attractive, shapely, and much too mature looking sixteen-year-old—

approached my desk. Then, looking over her shoulder at her friends in the corner, who seemed to be daring her to do it, she promptly sat upon my lap.

Dazed at first, it took me a couple of seconds to figure out what was happening and what to do. (There was no mention of such things in the employee handbook.) Normally I am not at all averse to attractive young women suddenly deciding to sit in my lap. But this was way different. I could hear a little voice in my head ask, What's wrong with this picture? Then, seconds later, the voice started screaming, "Stand up, stand up, you fool! I jumped from my chair, nearly dumping the girl on the floor as I mouthed some indignant protest. She just smiled and walked away.

As someone with no teaching experience, suddenly thrown into a classroom filled with unruly teenagers, I fared no worse than most first-year teachers, many of whom leave after only one year, vowing never to return to that infernal snake pit. Fortunately for me, the class sizes were small, and the kids were too emotionally messed up to notice what I was trying to teach anyway. I'm talking real heavy emotional issues. Kids hooked on drugs or suffering from various traumas. Kids who had been verbally and physically abused, often by their parents or other relatives. Many had even been sexually abused. They were shunted off to this school because their parents and their former schools could no longer deal with their problems. If this didn't work, the next stop was military school or an institution.

So there I was, a twenty-two-year-old guy, still screwed up in far too many ways, surrounded daily by a bunch of emotionally bleeding kids. Forget about the lesson plan. All they wanted was for me to listen. So I did.

In the process, I quickly realized that I was in no way equipped to handle this. I became too emotionally involved with these kids, talking with them frankly while trying to teach them a little science, but not having a clue how to help them.

I made it through the academic year and decided to leave, when the school offered me a limited, temporary contract due to financial uncertainties. Shortly thereafter, the school closed, though my decision probably had nothing to do with it.

After my ill-fated experience with teaching, I decided to try something else. A local pet shop was looking for a full-time sales associate. (Don't you love the way stores add that little word at the end to make the job sound more important?). This wasn't your run-of-the-mill pet shop, but an exotic pet shop. In addition to the usual puppies, birds, and tropical fish, they also sold critters like lizards, tarantulas, and snakes—my kind of animals. They liked the fact that I was a college boy and promised me that, if I worked really hard for two years and brownnosed the boss and didn't mind taking orders from his wife, who arrived each morning wearing more makeup than Alice Cooper, I would be promoted to assistant manager.

What I really wanted, however, was my first python, at full employee discount. He arrived at the shop one cold winter evening. A beautiful baby African rock python, he was only 18 inches long and perfectly gentle. I put him under my coat and brought him home to my parents' house and placed him in his cage, where he thrived and grew . . . and grew.

The problem with pythons as pets is that, with proper care, they can quickly begin to approach adult size, which in the case of a full-grown African rock python can be over twenty feet long, with a thick, muscular body used to constrict its prey.

Not only did my darling little pet quickly outgrow his cage, but he was now six feet long and quite a handful. Though still gentle as ever, there was always the danger in handling such a powerfully muscular snake that he might suddenly grow frightened of falling and wrap his coils around your neck for support, which is not conducive to breathing. In fact, that is exactly how they constrict and kill their prey. So sadly, I found him a new home and bid both him and the pet shop goodbye.

After that came a stint as a computer operator for an insurance company in Hartford. At the time, I knew nothing about computers–and still don't–but the hours seemed ideal. All I had to do was work three consecutive twelve-hour shifts from 7 p.m. to 7 a.m., and I had the rest of the week off. And for full-time pay and benefits. How tough could it be?

Basically, the job involved running large, room-sized computers called mainframes, which were series of various processing and communication units all hitched together and operated in batch mode. I was expected to keep them going, feeding them punch cards and magnetic tapes to run them at near full capacity while they spat out tests, insurance policies, statements, and payroll. I would then collect the continuous printed copy that came out. Scattered throughout the room were interactive terminals where you could push a button and make the computers pause in their operation.

One night, I was told by my shift supervisor to go hit a certain button. Now I knew perfectly well which button to push, having been instructed numerous times in proper button pushing. Turns out there was another button, way on the other side of the terminal console, which I think read "System Stop" and which was never, never to be pushed unless absolutely necessary. This button, you see, didn't just pause whatever operation was being run but shut down the whole system. Meaning that whatever programs had been running at the time had to be completely restarted, at considerable cost.

To this day, I still can't figure out why I pushed the wrong button. As soon as I hit it, I knew it was wrong.

Perhaps the subversion of my circadian rhythm and the cumulative lack of sleep had something to do with it. I remember a lot of yelling throughout the department, with people running around, looking for someone to blame, followed by the sound of laughter from my colleagues.

I was due for my annual performance review, the very next week. My boss, a kindly man whom I really liked, told me that I was doing great, overall, with top marks in all categories. Then he looked me straight in the face and shook his head. All he said was, "Why?"

Shortly after, I decided to pursue more normal work as a public schoolteacher, normal only in the sense that I was able to work during daylight hours. Despite the fact that my private school teaching had pretty much left me as much of an emotional wreck as the students I tried to teach, maybe I wasn't as bad a teacher as I thought. I took a few more college courses to get certified and to show I was serious. I was ready, or so I thought.

As it happened, there was an opening for a science teacher at the very same junior high school I had attended. I desperately needed a job and didn't give a second thought to any potential weirdness of going to work with my former teachers, including my much-feared, former Phys. Ed instructor, who had treated us worse than Marine recruits in boot camp.

The interview was a snap. The vice-principal and science department chairman briefly glanced at my

Forestry degree transcript, with a minor in philosophy. It was not especially heavy in hard science courses. However, they remembered that I had been an A-student and science nerd and hired me on the spot.

I was to teach Earth Science, which included geology, meteorology, and astronomy, to ninth grade students. As a kid, I had loved to collect rocks and gaze at the stars with my small telescope, so I was sure I could transmit that enthusiasm to my grateful, attentive students. Trouble was, I didn't know the first thing about either ninth-grade students or class control, which as I learned the hard way is just as important as knowledge of subject matter.

I shall not dwell here on the ugly details that still haunt my dreams. The kids were rude, disruptive, sneaky, and downright mean, constantly inventing new ways to torment and subvert me. In other words, they were perfectly normal, ninth-grade students. They ate me alive. A couple of times, the department chair who had hired me, upon hearing all the yelling and commotion coming from my classroom across the hall, came running into my room as if someone were being murdered. As soon as he entered, of course, the kids would all be sitting at attention, perfectly quiet. He would give me a disdainful look, then shake his head as he walked away muttering.

Bad as things were, at least I didn't have to worry about mass shooters. The worst event to happen was when one of my troubled students pulled a knife on a jock, right outside my classroom. We all ran out, and I momentarily froze. Then I herded my students to slowly back away. The issue was quickly resolved, as the jock yelled and threatened the student enough for him to drop his knife and run out the door. Show's over. No heroes, no deaths, that day.

I was a terrible teacher, but I made it through my first year. That was the main thing, the principal told me upon renewing my contract. "You survived." I had passed the test, and he expected me to carry on.

I worked there five more years, becoming a reasonably competent teacher, able to control the classroom while providing my students with a creative learning environment. I was now teaching seventh-grade life science and was given an expanded new science lab, which I lined with tropical plants and cages filled with snakes (including two boa constrictors), tarantulas, hissing roaches, and other exotic creatures. On Parents' Night, the principal would always show off my lab as a model classroom.

I did not delude myself into thinking I was a great teacher, however. During that time, I came to know some truly extraordinary teachers, fully attuned to their students and learning outcomes. But that would never be me. I had fallen into teaching because it offered a regular paycheck while aligning with my social and intellectual ideals, but my mind was elsewhere. And that's always a dangerous thing.

One day, one of the boys in my class called me out, openly challenging my authority. Something inside me snapped, and I suddenly shoved him up against the wall and shouted in his face. I watched myself, as if in slow motion, acting out this scene, and knew right then and there that I had to get out. (Can you imagine a teacher doing that in a public-school classroom today?)

There were many other jobs on the journey. None lasted more than five or six years. Yet, much like my character Lot O. Jobs, I saw each job as having its own flavor, providing new insights on life. I never wanted a big house or family, and fortunately neither did my wife, who found her niche early, pursuing a long career in education. So that left me free to follow my dreams, whatever the hell they happened to be at the time.

Some of the jobs, like groundskeeper and landscaper, involved down-and-dirty grunt work, even menial tasks, such as picking up trash. Others, like teaching and bookselling, required me to use my brain more than my back. Most of the jobs paid so little that, had it not been for my wife's job, I would have qualified for food stamps. What they lacked in remuneration, however, they repaid in new experiences and discoveries. It may sound corny, but through them, I found dignity in a day's labor and the simple joy of performing a job well. Mostly I was flying by the seat of my pants, learning as I went, though my final job–Instructional Specialist at the University of Arizona–made it sound as if I knew something. And when I left there, after working the usual five years, I actually did.

Through it all, writing remained the one constant thread. It was the one thing I really cared about. Since my twenties, I had dreamed of making a living from my creative writing, something that very few writers achieve. I did manage to find jobs as columnist, feature writer and editor at small local newspapers, and scored occasional sales of my stories, essays, and poems to magazines and newspapers–always the sweetest dollars earned–as I continued to feed the writing madness.

Maybe someday, I kept telling myself, if I do this long enough, I will make some real money from my writing. Yeah, right.

Meanwhile, I think back to all the jobs along the way, a rich tapestry which has given me enough raw material to last a lifetime–or at least to fill these pages–and to make a life from my writing.

WHERE THE MOOSE HAVE NO NAME

FOR SOME TIME NOW, I have resisted telling this story. In recounting events that began over forty years ago—a period since which I have lived many lives—it becomes increasingly difficult to separate fact from fiction. As the story gets replayed in my brain, it begins to take on its own reality shrouded in myth. The part about the schoolhouse I know is true, along with the hundred acres of forest that became an Audubon sanctuary. And there were definitely some moose involved.

Fortunately, I've been able to piece together some of the details from deeds still tucked away in a file. The story begins in 1976, barely a month after Josie and I were married. The White Mountains of New Hampshire had always been a magical place for me since childhood, and I had just purchased an eight-acre parcel of secluded forest land where I hoped we could eventually build a cabin. It was located on a dirt road in the rugged northeast corner of Landaff, a town which in 1980 had reached its lowest population of 266 people, though it has since rebounded to over four hundred.

The eight acres possessed all the essential qualities one could ask for in a White Mountains landscape, with a mixed forest of softwoods and hardwoods, moss-covered stone walls and boulders, and a merry mountain brook running through one corner. Josie was equally enchanted, as we continued to explore its hidden features while choosing possible sites to build our small cabin someday.

But just across the road trouble was lurking. Little did Josie know what a wild-eyed nature nut she had married. She knew I was an environmentalist, and was in fact moving in that direction herself. And she was fully aware of my mystical attachment to a nearby wooded area in Manchester, Connecticut, known as Case Mountain. During college, I had helped the town eventually preserve it as open space. Then, too, there was a certain craziness about me which she found appealing. But I don't think she was at all prepared for how crazy I could be when it came to land.

That summer, as we visited our eight acres, I happened to notice a "for sale" sign posted on the forest land across the road. Curious, I went over to inspect and entered a dense young stand of white pine, where the sun shone through canopy openings like green-tinted windows and I was greeted by the sweet sound of a rushing brook–a sound I've always found irresistible.

I called the phone number listed on the sign. The out-of-town owner informed us that the parcel was ninety-four acres and agreed to meet us next weekend and give us a tour if we were interested. We took him up on his offer, hoping he might be amenable to selling a much smaller piece directly across from our eight acres, with the idea of controlling the view from our future cabin. The idea of purchasing all ninety-four acres never entered my head.

The following Saturday morning, we met him as planned. A New Hampshire native, Edgar was a gentle, affable man who quietly led us around his land as he pointed out its features. There were no paths or trails. Instead, he took out a copy of an old survey map and followed the property boundaries as best he could, mumbling to himself and apologizing occasionally for forgetting which way to go.

As we slogged through dense dark swamps of balsam fir and spruce, past openings where a few large remnant white pines still stood after a recent logging operation, to a beaver pond near the back corner, then uphill through hardwood stands of white and yellow birch, aspen and beech which had seeded in after the Great Hurricane of '38, Josie and I remained largely silent as we slowly fell under the land's spell.

I finally broke the spell by asking, "So how much are you asking for it, Edgar?"

"Thirty-five thousand dollars," Edgar quickly replied,

then added, "but I'd be willing to finance it–up to fifteen years, if you like."

For a neophyte teacher and a budding school administrator just starting out in her first position, it seemed such a stunning amount–over $150,000 in 2018 dollars. And for what? Not a house, but a piece of undeveloped land on a dirt road. True, it was beautiful land, a magical property which engaged our senses with endless possibilities. We had walked only the boundary, yet it seemed to go on forever. What hidden surprises awaited our exploration? And to think it could be all ours, at a price of less than $400 per acre!

We politely thanked Edgar for the tour and told him we would have to think about it. Driving back home to our Connecticut apartment, it suddenly occurred to me that I had never bothered to ask him whether he might be willing to sell a smaller parcel of the land to us. But now the thought seemed almost sacrilegious. All we could think of was that boundless tract of wild land . . . if only we had $35,000.

That summer, we kicked it around, alternately doing the math to come up with a plan or trying to just forget about it. But the land had taken hold of us. And I came to realize something about my new spouse. Unlike her wild-eyed romantic husband, she was more practical and level-headed. But like me, she saw life as a continuing series of adventures, and this could be one of them. With the eight acres we already owned, we would be the owners of over a hundred acres of forest. But could we really afford it?

We couldn't, of course. It was absurd to even think about it. But come September of that same year, we signed a financing deal with Edgar and became the proud owners of 102 acres of forest land.

For the next couple of years, we spent most weekends and vacations visiting our new "baby." The fact that neither of us had wanted children meant that we could pool our emotional and financial resources into this new love affair. Yes, there were the monthly payments and taxes, but at least we didn't have to buy it new shoes or set up a college fund. I even spent a summer renting a cheap apartment in nearby Lisbon, during which I cleared hiking trails with a scythe while feeding my blood to the local black flies.

Josie and I spent hours walking the trails and discussing plans for the land. We delighted in showing off its natural features to friends and relatives curious about our strange new undertaking. Being educators, we began to see it as a place where we might share our love and knowledge of nature with the public. Thus was born the idea of a nature center. We began to lay plans for building a small house in the woods where someday we hoped to both live and conduct classes. Of course, the thought that our land happened to be in a semi-remote corner of northern New Hampshire where getting the public to visit might pose a problem never entered our heads.

Then, one day, as we drove past the little white house across from our land, we noticed a for sale sign. Known as the Scotland School, it was one of the original one-room schoolhouses in Landaff. (There was also an Ireland School, evidence of the wave of Scots-Irish immigrants who settled these parts and elsewhere in New England during the eighteenth century.) Located on a dirt road in the rugged, northeast corner of the town, it never had many students. Farming had always been difficult there and the population sparse. But for the few residents who did live there, Scotland School was its social heart.

We knew the owners, who ran a local natural foods store in nearby Franconia. They told us the price and showed us around. We gazed at the large quaint classroom with its venerable oak floor and large windows, some with their original wavy glass panes. Attached to the historic building was a tiny addition, all painted in red, with bay windows and woodstove. The owners had built it as an in-law apartment. It reminded us of a little dollhouse, set there beneath a large red maple tree.

All the way back to Connecticut, we couldn't stop talking about it. *Why, that place would make a perfect nature center. And just think, we wouldn't have to build one. There's even a little apartment we could live in someday. What's more, it's a living piece of history.* We weren't seriously thinking about it, of course, but it was fun to dream. And dreams don't cost anything, so long as you don't choose to act upon them.

But all that winter, the dream slowly grew into an obsession. Every time we visited our land, there was the schoolhouse, staring back at us through its two dark front windows. It was not the best time to be even thinking this. Josie had just decided to quit her administrative job to pursue her PhD, during which she would be paid all of $5,000 from a fellowship, while I attempted to keep us afloat with my meager teacher's salary. And we still had two loans to pay off for the land we had purchased. Financially speaking, there couldn't have been a worse time to consider it.

But the essential question boiled down to this: what if we lose it? It's so perfect for what we hope to do someday. The dream had taken complete control of our brains. We were like two hippie zombies. And that spring, we made an offer.

"So how much are they asking for this place?" said Ron, as he climbed out from the crawlspace beneath the old one-room schoolhouse we planned to buy. He was the local contractor we had hired to check out the building before making an offer.

"Thirty-seven five," I told him.

Ron shook his head and frowned. "I wouldn't pay

more than thirty grand, tops. Even that's too much." He pointed to the rough granite slabs of the foundation, several of which had shifted, allowing the oak floor to sag. Then he reminded me again of all the other stuff needing attention, including new roofing, glazing and repair of the old single-pane windows, and a badly needed paint job. Not to mention a host of other issues, including the lack of central heat (aside from two old woodstoves), a shallow dug well as the sole water supply, and a severely undersized septic system, all of which should have scared us off.

The fact that it didn't says much about the state of our heads at the time, suffering from an affliction causing a million other young and restless Americans–mostly white middle class and college-educated–during the '60s and '70s to flee the suburbs to seek their salvation in rural woods and fields. Known as the Back-to-the-Land movement, it would lead a young Jewish Brooklynite named Bernie Sanders to move to Vermont in 1968 where he purchased eighty-five acres of forest and renovated an old sugarhouse. And it would cause my sidekick Josie and I to leave good secure jobs in 1980 as teacher and administrator in a Connecticut suburban school system to take a flying leap into economic uncertainty in the wilds of northern New Hampshire.

So, in May of 1980, we purchased the schoolhouse and began our experiment in living. As Josie left for her dorm at the University of Connecticut to pursue her doctorate, at the last minute I had managed to secure a new position as science teacher in the Hardwick, Vermont school system. True, it did not pay as much as what I was currently making in Connecticut. But it was the closest job I could find–*only* fifty-seven miles–from our schoolhouse. Piece of cake, I thought, little realizing at the time how far that really was when you had to drive it every day, back and forth in our old Datsun, on a winding state highway, often covered with snow and ice, through lonely, unforgiving hills.

Perhaps I should tell you a little more about what kind of town we had bought into. Incorporated in 1774, Landaff had always been primarily a farming community, right on up into the 1940s. Soon after its founding, much of the less hilly land was cleared for cultivation, while the higher rugged slopes were stripped of their timber to become sheep pasture. By 1865, according to tax records, the number of sheep in town had grown to over five thousand. Farming was integral to residents. Social status was defined by your skill at farming. And of course, anyone who was anyone belonged to the local Grange. More on them later.

During the 1800s, as farming boomed, Landaff's population grew, to over a thousand by 1860. Twenty years later, with the loss of its eastern half to become the new town of Easton, its population dropped by half, and continued to drop as residents moved to more urban areas and word spread of richer, less stony land available in the West.

Perhaps its most famous resident was Harry Chandler, who was born there in 1864. As a young man, he moved to Los Angeles to seek his fortune. Arriving with barely a penny to his name, he eventually worked his way up to become the publisher of the *Los Angeles Times.*

Our first year was pretty much one of survival. While Josie pursued her doctorate in Connecticut, I established a beachhead in our new home and tried to hold things together. Our eventual plans for the land had to wait until our precarious financial situation improved. Most difficult of all was the realization that we would be able to see each other only two weekends a month, at best. Maybe that's why I still have such sweet memories of our sex life during those all too brief rendezvous, when it seemed as if we might never see each other again. Sometimes I would visit her on campus, where we would make love on the stiff mattress in her cramped dorm room and I felt like a college kid again.

Not wishing to be away from all the fun at the schoolhouse, eventually Josie purchased a big honking, beat up '67 Oldsmobile for $500 so she could come up more frequently. Every Sunday when she left, I would shudder to think of her driving back to Connecticut alone for four hours in that piece of junk, but for her it was just another adventure.

As Josie faced all the challenges of being a student

again, including research, writing, and eventually defending her dissertation, I tried to balance being on the road three hours of every day just to get to my new job and back. For a time, amidst the glory of the northern New England autumn foliage display and a couple of months before the snow began to turn the roads into icy death traps, it wasn't too bad. Hey, I can handle this, I thought. I tried to focus on the positive. Sure, I had to drive 114 miles each day, but I was driving through country straight out of a travel magazine, and at least I had a job.

But as the weather turned colder and snowier, a new reality set in. After work, I now had to juggle the daily tasks of feeding two woodstoves to keep warm and so our pipes wouldn't freeze, shoveling out a path through the snow to my car, and on some nights plugging in the engine so it would start in the morning. A suburban boy from Connecticut, I had never heard of such a thing. But when overnight temperatures plummet to ten or twenty below—even thirty below, one morning, when the air itself seemed to have frozen—you either plug in the engine block or you won't go anywhere.

More and more of my free time was spent in chopping firewood, shoveling snow, and keeping an anxious watch over our old house. During the interview for my teaching job in Vermont, the principal expressed concern over my long daily commute. I badly needed the job and assured him that I would get a small room in town where I could stay during the week and return home on weekends. Even as I said the words, I had no intention to do so. I was too scared of leaving our place alone for too long. Who knows what could happen? Burglars. Fire. Frozen pipes. Not to mention wild critters.

One cold night, I heard a strange gnawing sound, as if some giant mutant beetle were munching on the house from below. I went out to the passageway connecting our apartment to the schoolhouse, where it seemed to be coming from. In desperation, I threw a piece of sheet metal left over from a recent project hard against the floor, resulting in a loud metallic crash sure to frighten off any critter within miles. I listened. But the infernal munching continued. Finally, after several more such attempts, it suddenly stopped. I went inside and had another wine by the fire to soothe my jangled nerves.

Next day, after work, I inspected the foundation at the rear of the passageway and discovered a sizeable hole had been chewed straight through the plywood. I called Ron who, despite having done his best to dissuade us from buying the place was now all too glad to assist us with a never-ending list of repair projects. He pulled off a board and crawled underneath, where more chew marks and droppings were in evidence. "Looks like you have a porcupine," he said, in his usual quiet matter-of-fact manner, as if a porcupine eating your house was not at all out of the ordinary.

Apparently, porcupines love to chew on plywood, since the glue contains salt, a vital nutrient. It was just one of the many things we would learn during our sojourn in the White Mountains. Ron replaced the plywood footing, lining it with a barrier of sheet metal. Our porcupine problem was solved.

Other problems remained, but these would have to wait, as I faced my first full winter in residence. Some mornings, after a heavy snowfall, I would have to trudge through the snow and sweep off the car, hoping it would start, then slip and slide over unplowed roads to the highway. Of course, since I had to head for work hours before schools started–and a cell phone, even if there were such things back then, wouldn't have worked anyway–there was no way for anyone to reach me before driving the fifty-seven miles to Hardwick, where I would sometimes learn that school had been cancelled. All I could do was shrug and head back home, where I spent the rest of the day shoveling out a path for next morning.

Meanwhile, things were not going well in the classroom. I was seriously stressed out, wondering if I could take it any longer. All my thoughts were on our land and schoolhouse, and how to fake it as a teacher another day. Frequent disciplinary problems erupted, and I was not handling them well. But we could not afford for me to quit.

By April, things were looking up. Josie had secured a position as principal of a high school in Gray, Maine and would shortly be obtaining her doctorate. Since Gray was more than two hours from home and required that Josie secure a small apartment for the work week, we still faced a commuter marriage. But her increased salary meant that I could give up my teaching job and devote full time to what was turning into a lifestyle far more complex than either of us had dreamed. And we could start attending to the growing backlog of vital maintenance on our old schoolhouse.

I found a summer job with a nearby landscape company, and we began to plot our next moves. Over the next two years, there was the roof that desperately needed to be re-shingled. A new septic system. Windows that needed to be replaced or re-glazed. A water pump that needed to be wrapped in heat tape so it wouldn't freeze again in winter. Not to mention, the sagging oak floor. There was also the matter of a huge dying red maple that threatened the house, and the old framing of a partially built garage that had to be demolished. Its local bat inhabitants were not at all pleased.

Our plans for the nature center had to wait until the following summer. Meanwhile, as time permitted, we cleared hiking trails and chipped up debris left over from previous logging operations. Slowly a trail system began to emerge, and we started thinking about what kind of nature programs we would offer to the local public.

Our first program that summer included half a dozen

events, including a lecture on the history of the Scotland School by our new friend and local historian Stanley Currier. We still couldn't afford to pay anyone, but other friends graciously assisted us, curious about this new adventure of ours. Among these were two of our friends, Juan and Steve, topnotch naturalists and environmental educators from Connecticut, who led us on memorable nature walks through our little sanctuary. There was also our friend Mike, a herpetologist then employed at the New York Museum of Natural History, who gave a slide talk on northern New Hampshire reptiles and amphibians, and excitedly informed us of finding specimens of the large salmon-colored northern spring salamander in Scotland Brook. We found that people were glad to freely share their expertise with the public, even though their audiences were disappointingly sparse, at times.

Josie and I also led occasional classes on wildflowers and other subjects. Our land became a place for us to engage our passion for nature study as never before, perhaps because nature was right there, in our backyard. We learned all the names of local trees, shrubs, ferns, and wildflowers, including those of the ten species of native orchids we "discovered" there. We tracked the local wildlife and were thrilled, one winter, to see the tracks of a fisher and what looked like those of a lynx following the tracks of the abundant snowshoe hares. We read the claw marks of bears on trees and rotting stumps, and the telltale holes of pileated woodpeckers.

Then, one winter, we discovered the droppings and tracks of what had to be either the biggest damn white-tailed deer that ever lived or a . . . moose. Could it be? We had always thought of moose as wilderness animals, more associated with northern Maine or Canada. Portions of the surrounding White Mountains of New Hampshire were pretty wild, but not that wild, we thought. As far as we knew, moose were known to occur only in the extreme northern part of the state. But there had been tantalizing recent reports in the newspapers of occasional moose sightings in both nearby Vermont and New Hampshire.

One cloudy winter afternoon, while hiking the local Bronson Hill behind our house, I came upon some fresh tracks in the snow. Moose tracks. I fetched my camera and followed them. And suddenly there she was, in full moose living color, together with two calves. She turned to face me, warily eying this reckless male creature stalking her. I approached as close as I dared, snapped a few quick photos, then backed away slowly, as awareness of my danger began to trickle into my brain. It was a stupid thing to do, and I would not have blamed her at all if she had charged and trampled me.

In the next few months, we started to see moose everywhere, sometimes even using the very trails we had constructed. One fall morning, I looked out the window and couldn't believe my eyes. There, in the middle of the front yard, stood a female moose. Whether it was the same individual whose domain I had invaded the previous winter I can't say. With a look of detached curiosity as if checking us out, she briefly peered at me through the window. Then calmly she headed back into the alder thicket from which she had emerged. The whole experience lasted only a minute or two, but it left a lasting image and a priceless reminder of why we were living there.

We initiated a membership campaign, inviting people, for an annual small fee, to join our mission of sharing a greater knowledge and appreciation of the natural world. Eventually we grew to over a hundred members, mostly from the local area and Connecticut. Though small, the number still surprised us. The fact that there were so many people who believed in us and wanted us to succeed touched our hearts.

I also started writing more, mostly about the natural features to be seen at our doorstep. After observing the moss-covered blowdown on the back hillside of our land and noting the way it all pointed in roughly the same direction as a result of the '38 hurricane, I wrote a brief essay about our changing forest and submitted it to a local weekly shopper. The result was my first paid writing assignment, a weekly nature column called "Nature's School" which would continue for the next few years.

While studying and adapting to our local environment

and its inhabitants, we also tried to fit in with the people in our community. Very much aware of the suspicion that many locals had of us, we did our best to reach out and become part of the social scene. Whenever we could, we engaged people in conversation, trying to bridge our differences and find common ground. Some would not be dissuaded, we realized, despite our best efforts. We would always be those two hippie environmentalists, especially that crazy, long-haired, bearded fella who still uses hand tools to cut wood and is always going on about birds and wildflowers.

The local hunters viewed us with particular disdain, especially after we began posting our land as an environmental education area, where hunting and trapping were not permitted. As one disgruntled hunter finally explained to me, parts of our land were particularly prized by locals as one of the best areas to shoot snowshoe hares, and they viewed our posting as an act of war. Rural natives generally frown upon posting of any kind on forested land, insisting that it should remain open to the public for all kinds of recreation, especially hunting.

One late night, we were awakened by the sound of loud voices and baying hounds. Grabbing a flashlight, I followed the sound up the road back of our house that led to Bronson Hill. I came across a motley band of hunters who, with the aid of their hounds, were out hunting racoons. Though tired and pissed off at being awakened by what seemed to me an ungodly intrusion into my private space, I did my best to politely inquire exactly what the fuck they were doing at this hour of the night as they kept from bursting out laughing at the sight of this indignant city slicker. One of them did manage to hold it in long enough to politely explain, and in the process, I learned way more than I wanted about the so-called sport of chasing and treeing a raccoon.

During hunting season, especially when the sound of gunshots seemed near, I would don bright clothing and head out to patrol the boundaries of our land. Nervously, I would carry an ax, as if I were out performing some clearing task. Not that I was trying to provoke an incident. But these were men carrying guns–I never met a female hunter–and I was not about to go out and face them without something in my hand, even if it seemed faintly ridiculous. Whenever I encountered a hunter on our land, I would go up to him and introduce myself. I would ask if he knew that this was posted land and that it was being used for educational and research purposes. Sometimes we would strike up a conversation, and he would tell me about how his family had hunted this land for generations. And I would tell him about the activities of our little nature center. Not that I hoped to change his mind. But I felt it was important for me to reach out, and though some of our signs were still torn down from time to time, the number of shell casings and gun shots eventually diminished.

In time, more local citizens began to attend our programs. Our overall public approval rating had increased considerably by the fact that Josie had just secured a position as the regional Superintendent of Schools, overseeing not only our little school system but that of all the surrounding towns. One of us, at least, now held a respectable job.

Josie and I still wanted to do more to make us feel part of the community. Several of our new friends invited us to become members of the local grange. A few words are in order here. The Grange, or The National Grange of the Order of Patrons of Husbandry as it is officially called, is a fraternal organization which seeks to promote the economic and political well-being of the community and agriculture. Among their stated goals are: "To develop a better and higher manhood and womanhood among ourselves" and "to foster mutual understanding and cooperation." How can you argue with that? Though I think the goal to "earnestly endeavor to suppress personal, local, sectional, and national prejudices, all unhealthy rivalry and all selfish ambition" struck me as quaintly quixotic.

It sounded harmless enough, so we decided to give it a try. If we had known, however, that these goals are expressed through solemn rituals and ceremonies based on Roman and Greek mythology, Freemasonry, and Christian beliefs, and even a secret password, we might have changed our minds. I hate rituals of any kind, but it was too late.

We tried to be good sports, immersing ourselves in the initiation ceremony while dutifully repeating the oaths. Luckily it did not involve donning animal costumes or renouncing our families, though there was a thing about referring to our fellow members as brothers and sisters. We faithfully paid our dues, planned and attended long meetings, though it got old after a while. It's amazing the things people will do to fit in.

Meanwhile, it was becoming increasingly apparent to both of us that we could never be fully a part of this local community. People were friendly enough, but there just weren't enough of them in this tiny burg to make it seem like a real town. Too many of them, proud of their native heritage, subscribed to a stony sense of self-reliance and fierce devotion to custom and their inner circle. No matter what we did or how long we lived there, we would always be considered outsiders.

Our social isolation was taking its toll on both of us, but especially me. Recent trips to Boston and New York City to visit friends and relatives made me more aware than ever of all the rich cultural experiences we were missing in choosing to live here. At least Josie had the daily chance to interact with the public, while I mostly interacted with various small mammals, birds, toads, and an occasional moose. The only thing that saved me were our public programs and the infrequent visitor. At least I got to do the weekly grocery shopping in Littleton, a fifteen-mile drive and the only sizeable nearby town, where I could hobnob with the locals in the produce aisle. Then too, there was the mailman, who always had time to chat, and the loquacious owner of the drugstore, who pontificated freely on issues of the day for anyone who dared to listen.

Though she enjoyed her job, Josie increasingly had to deal with the parochialism so common to rural schools. Little by little, we began to contemplate the unthinkable. When we first moved here, I thought it would be that magical place of my dreams, the place where we would sink our roots firmly and grow our life together. Having risked so much to be here, I couldn't imagine ever leaving.

Josie, on the other hand, never contemplated living in just one place for the rest of her life. Ever the realist, she saw better than I could the downside of remaining here too long and the effect it was starting to have on me. "What do you want to do?" she asked.

We both fiercely loved this place and didn't relish the prospect of leaving. For us, it was a one-of-a-kind, deeply spiritual adventure. Indeed, the land had become almost sacred to me. My whole identity and reason for being were intimately tied up with it. If I knew back then how wrenching the experience of our separation would later prove to be for me, I might have never found the courage to move.

Month by month, the feeling that we had to do something only intensified. Finally, one Sunday morning, it all became crystal clear while scanning *The Boston Globe* classifieds. The want ads were full of positions for School System Superintendent (a number that has since only multiplied for this increasingly thankless, impossible job). And I had just made my first sale of a children's story to *Highlights for Children*, one of the top fiction markets in the country. Suddenly it all seemed doable. Josie shrugged and said what both of us were thinking, "Well, are you ready for a new adventure?"

But the problem of what to do with our sanctuary and schoolhouse remained. We couldn't stand the thought of just selling them like so much real estate, especially the land. Cleared for sheep, stripped of its second and third growth timber, bought and exchanged for investment by multiple owners, it had suffered many changes. We wished to protect it somehow, to give it a chance to heal without having to serve some limited economic purpose. But then, how would we pay off our mortgage and two property loans?

Fortunately, well before any thoughts of moving, we had developed a new working relationship with The Audubon Society of New Hampshire, which now goes by the name of New Hampshire Audubon. We had agreed to an educational partnership between them and our Scotland School Environmental Center. The more we worked with them, the more we realized how closely our goals meshed. Then an idea occurred. Would they be interested in our land as one of their statewide sanctuaries?

We were visited by a small committee of board members along with then Executive Director Les Corey. Together we walked the land, recalling that time which now seemed long ago when we had first walked the land with Edgar. They marveled at all the work we had put in on the trails and the variety of wildlife habitats, as Josie and I shared all the special corners and stories of this land we had come to cherish. It didn't take the committee long to decide that it would make a fine wildlife sanctuary.

We proposed to donate the property to New Hampshire Audubon with the understanding it would become one of their sanctuaries. We also agreed that it would not be named after us, but instead after Scotland Brook that flowed through a portion of the land. Though we could not afford to donate our schoolhouse, as part of the deal we agreed to grant them first refusal to purchase it as an educational facility.

In a short time, we received our answer. New Hampshire Audubon would gladly accept our donation. However, they declined our offer to purchase the house, which left us no choice but to list it on the market.

As I look back on it now, the exact timing of the deal and the way it all managed to come together still amazes me. But I know we did finally donate the land and have the old deeds to prove it. Josie had secured a position as

Superintendent of Schools in North Kingstown, RI, and reluctantly we sold our schoolhouse, for an amount more than our asking price. Mortgage and loans were paid off. Barely six years after we had first moved there—a period that seemed like a lifetime—we were landless and near penniless, heading off to a new adventure in Rhode Island.

But we faced a new challenge—explaining our action to both our parents.

First to hear the news was my dad. "You mean you just gave it away?" He eyed his hopelessly idealistic son, then his new daughter-in-law, with her new PhD, whom he thought was more level-headed. Then he shook his head sadly and sighed.

Then it was Josie's mother, who got straight to the point. "What, are you crazy? I thought you bought that land as an investment. You're not exactly rich, you know. You could have made a bundle, if you just held on to it for a while."

In hindsight, I must admit it was a pretty crazy thing to do. Having paid off the mortgage and loans, we had almost nothing left from the sale of our schoolhouse. And here we were, setting off on a new adventure. We would be starting from scratch, with nothing to show for it. Nothing, that is, but six years of memories and the knowledge that our hundred acres would always be there, preserved for those who came after us to view its wild orchids or birds or walk quietly on woodland trails through upland forests laced with ferns and old stone walls.

Since then, there have been many new adventures and places to call home. And now that we live in Arizona, "our" sanctuary sometimes seems far away, as if it might as well be on Mars. On my desk is a small piece of granite from the streambed of Scotland Brook so I can reach out and squeeze its crystalline firmness to remind me of another reality. Our trips to New England have become less frequent, and whenever we've managed to revisit this special landscape, I always find myself wondering if this time might be the last.

During our most recent visit, we had the good fortune of meeting local Audubon volunteers Joanne and Kevin, who have adopted the sanctuary as their own, keeping the trails cleared and much more. When we reached the parking lot, it was raining. We decided to take a short hike anyway. But first, Joanne and Kevin had a little surprise for us.

There, mounted on a new kiosk for all to see was a poster they had designed. Accompanied by a map and photographs, it tells the story of Scotland Brook Wildlife Sanctuary and its many features to see and explore. At that moment, I almost lost it. In a flash, everything became clear. For us, it was the only thing we could have done. The proof was standing in front of me, with these two dedicated people who continue to carry out our dream.

As we slogged through the wet woods, Joanne and Kevin showed us their good work while pumping us with questions, like if we remembered where an old trail used to go or where a certain species of orchid could be found. We drew a blank on many of their questions. In a way, it seemed as if we were seeing this landscape anew, as on that first day when we walked the land with Edgar. Thirty-two years had passed since we moved away and much had changed. Trails had been rerouted and improved, with wooden walkways installed, courtesy of nearby high school students. The local Ammonoosuc Chapter of New Hampshire Audubon sponsored periodic "Trail Days" to clear the trails of blowdown and brush. At a glance, it was the same forest we remembered, but in our absence, trees had grown and openings had filled in. Overall, the forest appeared healthy, with few signs of die-off or decline. In particular, I remarked how some of the big white pines left over from logging now seemed bigger and more prominent than before. It's amazing how fast white pines can grow in thirty years, on an optimal site. Of course, part of the reason they seemed more impressive, as Joanne and Kevin explained, may have also had something to with the fact that another local Audubon volunteer, Dave, had recently cleared out the undergrowth around their trunks to better show them off.

As we returned to the parking lot, I noticed that the poster included a quote from a nature column that I had written back then about our changing White Mountain forests: "There is a tremendous resilience to our forests. It is the resilience of alder growing on an otherwise bare rock slide or a tough sapling sprouting through a crack in an abandoned field or aspen and cherry quickly invading a fire-blackened site. It is the resilience of nature which always abhors a vacuum and rushes in to fill the openings left by its own vagaries or those of humans." Resilience is a fitting word to describe how this little patch of forest continues to grow and change in response to both historic and natural processes. But there is a new challenge facing it today, caused not by nature or previous land use patterns, but as a direct result of an historically unprecedented, anthropocentric climate change the likes of which these woods and nature have never seen.

We sometimes think of nature as some grand and unmovable force independent of our puny efforts to control it. In his seminal 1989 book *The End of Nature*, Bill McKibben writes: "Nature, we believe, takes forever. It moves with infinite slowness throughout the many periods of its history"

But now, within the geologically miniscule time frame of centuries, we have become deadly volcanoes, spewing enough carbon dioxide into the air from the burning of fossil fuels to literally change the atmosphere. "The temperature and rainfall are no longer to be entirely the work of some separate, uncivilizable force," writes McKibben, "but instead in part a product of our habits, our economies, our ways of life."

I wrote my column about our changing forest years before McKibben's book came out. When I first read it, like many readers I did not want to believe in the idea that we could so alter the atmosphere as to change the course of natural events. Since then, the scientific evidence for his thesis has become incontrovertible, except to a shrinking group of deniers whose avarice and willful ignorance shall be judged harshly by future generations. Meanwhile, projected worldwide changes and events that once seemed farfetched now occur with alarming frequency.

The reports from New Hampshire are not good. Most of the state has warmed two to three degrees F. in the last century. Spring arrives earlier and fall later. Winters are shorter and warmer, with less snow and more rain. Warmer summers bring drought and increasing hot and dry conditions. Extreme weather events become more common during all seasons, with winter thaws followed by intense cold, and heavier rainstorms more frequent.

Superficially, the woods we walked through that day looked the same to me, but year by year they are changing. What they will look like in fifty or a hundred years is anyone's guess. All I can say for certain is that the Scotland Brook Wildlife Sanctuary we once knew will be a very different place in the future.

Whether its moose will survive is questionable. During

the 1800s, there were fewer than fifteen moose left in New Hampshire. Today there are so many moose that the state had to institute an annual hunt to reduce the herd to prevent moose-car collisions. But with increasingly warmer winters and hotter summers, favorable habitat for moose is likely to decrease. Meanwhile, winter ticks are increasing. It is estimated that 70 percent of moose calves are dying each year as a result. An adult moose can often be infested with thousands of ticks. Imagine a thousand ticks on you at once, all sucking your blood.

Will there still be snowshoe hares, I wonder, as deep winter snows become less frequent? Will the same warblers return each spring, or will new species take their place?

Will the hemlocks die off as a result of the invasive wooly adelgid, a sucking insect slowly expanding northward? Will our beloved sugar maples, yellow birches, balsam firs, and red spruces vanish, as these species retreat to higher elevations? Will there still be trees at all or will mass die-offs from insects or disease leave nothing but graveyard forests to incinerate as raging wildfires become the new reality?

Will there still be ten species of orchids, or none? Will there be wood frogs in the wet meadows? Will the Scotland Brook still flow through the pine woods?

For Josie and me, establishing the sanctuary was an unabashedly sentimental, defiant act—an investment in a future we will never know. But what happens when the natural forest we loved and sought to preserve no longer exists? Nature will still exist, of course, as it always has, even if greatly diminished, as it was during the Great Permian Extinction–or Great Dying–when most of the world's life became extinct. Life will still go on at Scotland Brook, even if it takes some form we cannot imagine. But will it still be a place where people come to walk and experience its natural beauty? And will there still be a New Hampshire Audubon Society or some group like it to protect and manage it? I'd like to think so. Perhaps McKibben is right in that "there is no future in loving nature," or at least the nature we once knew. For that nature is gone, robbed of its rich diversity by those who turned a blind eye to science. But for as long as our species manages to survive, I think there will always be some of us who will go on loving nature and finding delight in whatever forms it takes.

Scotland Brook is just one small place within that precious sanctuary we call Earth. You must forgive a sentimental old man for worrying too much about what happens to a tiny forest in New Hampshire as, year by year, thousands of species now go extinct and entire ecosystems are threatened. Millions of people are losing their homes or dying from extreme weather-related events such as flooding, heat stress, wildfires, increased air pollution, and the spread of insect vectors and diseases. Whether humans eventually find a way to deal with climate change and prove as resilient as nature itself does not look promising, as greenhouse emissions continue to rise, politicians dither, and fossil fuel lobbyists lie and deny.

At this point, I'd say the moose, ticks and all, have a better chance.

THE PIPE IN THE CLOSET

A RECENT NIGHTMARE GOT ME thinking about it again. It was a creature feature short. I was paid a visit by James Arness–not as the reassuring Western hunk of his *Gunsmoke* days but as that darkly disturbing alien hulk portrayed in *The Thing from Another World.* He was trying to come through our front door. Lacking an M-1 rifle or even a modest flamethrower (neither of which, come to think of it, worked all that well in the movie), I hit his arm with the only weapon at hand–a book. I can't recall the title, but it didn't slow him down in the least. I tried another and another, but he kept right on coming. Just as that awful hand was about to clutch my throat . . . I woke up. There was no monster, except perhaps the one staring back at me from mirrored closet across the room. And it was then that I remembered that other thing that still resides there.

A handy piece of iron pipe, about three feet long had been in that closet ever since we'd bought our house in Providence, Rhode Island. The only time it wasn't there was during a brief period of bedroom remodeling. That would have been a good time to remove it from my life, once and for all, but no. Quietly I put it back, obeying some strange impulse. And there it sat in the darkness, waiting to do my bidding.

As to what I would actually do with this pipe, I'm not sure. I can just imagine myself, faced with some nocturnal alarm, reaching for my weapon from the place where it has always been. With two shaky hands I will grasp and absorb its iron strength. Fierce and invincible like a great Lithuanian knight of old, I will swish it about. And most likely, I will smash the closet mirror, drop the pipe on my toes and pass out on the floor.

Admittedly, it is not the best home security system. The fact that I considered one at all is just one of the many psychological adjustments one makes in moving to an urban neighborhood. In our former suburban and country digs, the possibility of some drug-crazed, homicidal maniac trying to break down our front door had always seemed a remote one. Now it doesn't seem quite as unlikely, thanks to daily police reports along with the occasional grim rumor from skittish neighbors. But this was our new home. My wife and I had chosen to live here because it offered us an environment more stimulating than the cloistered purity of the countryside or the boring nothingness of the suburbs. Part of that stimulation, however, as with life in general, comes from our awareness of the dark side–that we share the same streets, rubbing elbows with a few individuals whose backgrounds and values are so vastly different from our own as to think nothing of bashing in our front door, or worse, to rob us of what little wealth and peace of mind we still possess.

This is not to suggest we spent our nights cowering in the living room, with all the lights on, awaiting some cold, cruel visitor. We took reasonable precautions, such as installing dead bolt locks (and remembering to use them) and not leaving any money, furs, or jewelry on the front porch.

Once, however, we did consider taking more drastic measures, though not quite as drastic as that in a newspaper ad. Beneath a picture of a "395 security system"–a handgun, actually–the ad promoted a popular electronic system that is both cheaper and more effective, since the gun "can't call the police." That is the trouble with handguns. They aren't very smart. They can't do much of anything except to hurl a bullet, when squeezed, into the living body of some person, quite often the wrong person. But such is the price of security, some would say.

And the trouble with at least some electronic security systems is that they *do* call the police, over and over, like the boy who cried wolf. Or they inflict their raucous signals on entire neighborhoods, shattering the peace far more effectively than any heavy metal music. Having to live with these noxious car and house alarms, which seem to go off at the slightest change in temperature or humidity, and most frequently in the wee hours of deepest, hard won slumber, I would almost prefer that the owners of these infernal contraptions just stick their heads out the window and scream as long as they pleased. At least it would be more human than the electronic whine that slices through my spine like a filet knife. And the screams would stop a whole lot quicker, I suspect, than the eternity it takes a siren to be turned off. As for me, I would rather not own such things as require an alarm, having more than enough alarms in my life already. Indeed, I would rather have all my worldly possessions stolen right out from under me than to inflict such torture upon my good neighbors.

Yet, as the security ad reminds us, "one in four American homes is victimized by crime." So, what are we to do?

Well, we could buy a dog, says my buddy from Boston, a victim of one too many break-ins. Get one that barks at the sound of leaves falling. Not a yap, mind you, but a full-throated, hound from the moors kind of bark–one that would make an intruder think twice. But since nearly every house in our neighborhood, not to mention the city, already seems to have at least one canine inhabitant, why bother? If I got a dog, even a dog that barked every second, who would notice? The only thing one might notice in our neighborhood would be the sudden sound of no barking.

Which brings me back to my pipe. While it may seem primitive or foolish to some, there is much to recommend it. First of all, it's cheap. Ours was left there by the previous owners. I wonder if they, too, kept it there for a similar reason. Also, it doesn't require bullets or electricity. And no maintenance is ever required, except perhaps an occasional light coat of Rustoleum.

Furthermore, there are no buttons to push. No codes or instructions to forget. Picking up a pipe, or as in the case of our fossil ancestors, a club, is not something you easily forget. We've had pipes in our closets and caves far too long to forget.

This violent, primitive image of myself does give me pause, however. Why do I, a grown man, still feel the need to keep a pipe in his closet? As a boy, I played with wooden swords and toy guns. Later, as a young man, I played with real knives and guns, indulging my Western fantasies. Fortunately, I grew out of them before hurting anyone. Yet the pipe's still there.

I suppose the pipe represents some last vestige of primal reaction to an ancient and very real fear. Would I actually use it if the time comes? Who can say? Perhaps, rather than marching down the stairs to confront the attacker, I will merely hide under the covers or, better yet, send my wife down in my place. But one thing I know. If I do go down those steps alone, I must have something in my hands. I am just not strong enough to face the midnight terror unarmed.

I must have my prop to convince me at least, if not the attacker, that I will defend our home with the proper fervor. But a book, even the most ponderous tome of metaphysics, simply will not do. And neither will a gun, for then I might actually shoot someone, and that is a price I will not pay. I'll grab my trusty pipe instead. If forced to use it, and most likely I will, for then it won't be a shot in the dark but a last-ditch attempt at survival. Not that I would get to use it. Someone determined or crazy enough to break into our house will not be deterred by the sight of a middle-aged man in his underwear with a pipe. He'll probably laugh till he cries, then calmly kill me. But at least I won't wake up the neighbors.

ROMANCING THE STONES

IT WAS 1989, AND THEIR North American "Steel Wheels" tour was coming to an end as rock critics filled the news and air waves with adjective-strewn accounts of this greatest of all rock 'n' roll bands. What follows is one man's attempt to look beyond the hoopla and deal with the emotional aftermath of having been a witness to this phenomenon known as The Stones.

Actually, you don't need a "the." Stones will suffice. It's the same with Grand Canyon, as a native Arizonan once told me. Stones. Grand Canyon. There is only one.

For those expecting some penetrating analysis of Stones music, read no further. I am as far from being a rock critic as Barry Manilow is from being a heavy metal musician, though that might be interesting. I almost didn't write anything at all about my experiences at the Sullivan Stadium concert in Foxboro, after reading local columnists' stories. How could I hope to match Maria Miro Johnson's moving description of my favorite member of the group? "There was Keith Richards, his face as lined as a river bed, and with a headband around his skull, like some aerobics instructor from hell." Or Janice Page's inspired observation: "Richards always sang like he was gargling razor blades." Pure poetry.

Furthermore, I'm not what you might call a certified Stones fan. I have difficulty keeping all their names straight (Mick is the one with the tongue, right?) and can seldom produce on demand any vital Stones statistics, such as which former member was found dead of a drug overdose at the bottom of his swimming pool. (I know it's not Keith. He only looks like he's dead.) I don't have all thirty-four of their albums and couldn't for the life of me sing more than a few words from any of their tunes. What kind of fan is that?

Before that year, in fact, I had never attended a Stones concert, and thought I never would.

Of course, like anyone whose blood rushes at the sound of real rock 'n' roll, I am a devoted fan. Even during their mercifully short disco phase, the group has always been true to a no-nonsense, down-and-dirty kind of music, against which few other rock groups can compete. And that is about as far as I dare to go about riveting power chords and other such rock talk without revealing my wholesale ignorance in these matters.

But when a tune like *Honky-Tonk Women* or *Brown Sugar* gets played, even when it's played badly, there is never any doubt about whether it's real rock 'n' roll or, for that matter, what to do about it. Something snaps in the brain, and our hips begin to sway as we chant the words to our anthem. Ask any DJ or top forty rock band the best way to get a bunch of inhibited, two left feet people out onto the dance floor. Just play a Stones tune (though preferably not one of their early blues pieces or countryish ballads). As if by magic, every square foot of space will be instantly filled with jumping, stomping, elbow-jabbing enthusiasts, most of whom wouldn't normally be caught dead on a dance floor.

Sometimes Josie and I would go out dancing at which times we resembled not so much Fred and Ginger as a couple of desperate lemmings, answering some unknown, primitive urge. It was usually a Saturday night thing. Abetted by our two crazy friends, Dan and Yvonne, we followed the rhythm of something as old as humans. No ballroom dancing for us. Just the chance to hear some of that good old-fashioned, foot stomping rock 'n' roll and, if the music was right, to get out onto the dance floor and perform some nameless, shuffling, shaking kind of rite which our earliest ancestors would surely have recognized.

It used to be that I always had to have a few drinks before venturing out on the dance floor. This goes back to my senior year at college, the first time I dared to dance. It was one of those Friday night mixers. Goaded by friends to overcome my stupid inhibitions, and yet too painfully shy and self-conscious, I had to get myself so drunk that I could barely stand before I would dare step out onto that stage of public humiliation. No doubt, the band played a few Stones tunes, though I remember little of that night, except the fact that I was dancing for the first time.

Ever since then, though still feeling the occasional urge for an alcoholic nudge, I no longer have to get drunk to dance. In fact, the moment I first realized that there is something strangely magical about Stones music was when, one night, I found myself out on the dance floor prancing around like Mick to one of their songs and it dawned on me that I was stone-cold sober. From that moment on, I was a true believer.

This is not to say that I was a Stones purist. I still tried to keep up on at least a few of the new rock groups and liked a lot of the stuff played on MTV. I also loved Led Zeppelin and AC/DC. But there is something about Stones music that goes straight for my emotional jugular. With some pieces, it's more the music than the lyrics, but when they both work the effect is magical. I knew I was still among the living when my spirit could be stirred to such heights. It is not something I can explain. But one does not have to understand why something moves you. The only important thing is that it still does.

Back in 1981, I was living in the wilds of New Hampshire. When I read the news that the Stones were scheduled to appear as part of their American Tour at the Hartford Civic Center on November 9 and 10, to promote their new album *Tattoo You*, I immediately called my little sister and instructed her to run out and buy me a ticket. (Note to younger readers: Back in those days, you couldn't buy a ticket online. You couldn't buy *anything* online, for the simple fact that the Internet didn't become available to the public until 1991.) I told her that she might have to stand in line all night, but if she truly loved me, she would do it. She laughed and told me to get a life. It was the last North American tour the Stones would do until 1989. So much for ever seeing the Stones. That night, I played one of their tapes and wept bitterly into my gin-and-tonic.

In the years that followed, Josie and I would often sit around with the other members of our local fan club, Dan and Yvonne, and discuss whether our band would ever tour again. After all, the Stones were pushing forty, and so were we. It seemed impossible. Nonetheless, we made a solemn pact that, should our dream come true, we would see the Stones together.

Over the years, I kept pumping Dan, who in his younger days had been a pretty mean rocker himself, for inside information. "What do you think, Dan? Are they ever gonna do it?" Dan would simply shrug and flash an impish Alfred E. Neuman grin. At least *he* had seen the

Stones, the lucky bastard.

So when the first rumors started trickling in about Mick and Keith trying to bury the hatchet, working on another album and–wonder of wonders–*going on tour*, I was cautiously skeptical After all, Mick was still off somewhere doing his own thing, and Keith had just come out with his own first solo album. The group hadn't done a live show in seven years, and it was, in fact, their longest concert drought. When Josie bought me a copy of Keith's album, I almost returned it in disgust. I hadn't bought any of Mick's albums and I wasn't about to buy into Keith's. Neither one of them alone could ever replace the Stones. In the end, I decided to keep the album, partly because of Keith's gravelly voice which sounds so bad it ends up good, but also because in his own erratic way he was trying to find some fresh approaches to the kind of music that he and the band had always played.

But when news came out that Mick and Keith were off in Barbados, writing songs for a new album and, shortly later, that the group was hiding out and practicing in a rural retreat in Connecticut, I started to believe the impossible. Here I was, forty-one, and here they were, back again.

As if I needed any further reminder of the incredible series of events beginning to unfold, my dad, who collects *Life* magazines, handed me a precious copy of the July14, 1972 issue (which, now that I think about it, I could have sold for a bundle at the concert), whose cover shows a bare-chested Mick Jagger strutting his stuff, with the caption "The Stones are Rolling Again." I was amused not only by the photos but by the opening remarks written by Thomas Thompson: "The Rolling Stones! Are they still among us? How can they be? In history's first disposable society, where everything from graceful landmarks to diapers to rock groups is used and thrown away, how can the Stones survive? In a decade—ten years!—of performing, they have earned some of the worst press clippings since Mussolini."

I especially liked that part about Mussolini. Thompson went on to reflect on what, even then, were the legendary antics of these bad boys of rock, from their scarlet stuck out tongue trademark to the infamous Altamont concert where a young man was stabbed to death at the foot of the stage by one of the Hells Angels hired that night for—yes—security. The writer reminded me all too well of my mixed emotions on being a Stones believer. For there is a dark downside that comes from persistently going for the throat. Stones music, at its best, is a primal, crunching, crouching sort of thing. It toys with us like a black cat playing with a mouse. It plays to our inner darkness and fascination with evil, yet triumphs in the end, like all blues-based music, in the fact that we manage to survive in spite of it all.

Josie reminded me of this negative aspect as we listened, one night, to their song "Under My Thumb" from the *Aftermath* album. The song relates a sexual power struggle about finally gaining control over a once pushy woman, who's now a "squirmin' dog who's just had her day" and becomes his sweet pet. We discussed the sexual politics of a man who could write such offensive lyrics. "Everyone changes," I weakly offered.

"Yeah, sure," replied Josie, icily. Just look at the kind of women he and the others hang out with, and how they treat them all like their little play things." I shut up as my hand kept tapping out the driving beat to "Under My Thumb."

And now here they were again, my grinning bad boys, on the cover of the September 4, 1989 issue of *Time* magazine, which gave them a respectability that, ironically, another magazine called *Rolling Stone* never could. The Stones were rolling again.

I still didn't have any tickets, though. I had assumed that Dan, with all his old Boston rock band connections, would take care of this, maybe even get us behind the stage.

But in the end, it was my own outrageous Lithuanian good fortune that came through. I had heard that the Stones would be doing three concerts at Foxboro, beginning Friday, September 29.

No longer secluded in the wilds of New Hampshire,

I was now living in Providence. On the very morning the tickets were scheduled to go on sale, I happened to be in Harvard Square on my way to work. As I went up the stairs from the subway, I eyed a handwritten sign for Rolling Stones tickets at the Out-of-Town Ticket Agency. Already a small line had formed. Turns out, they were only accepting deposits of $30 each ticket (and $10 more on delivery). I immediately plunked down $60, for which I received a little slip of paper (which said virtually nothing except the fact that I'd paid $60), then ran to the bank and came back with $60 more–just in case my buddy Dan didn't come through.

Then I waited. I read the horror stories of people waiting in line all night at various Ticketron outlets, only to be issued a stupid wristband and told they now had to wait in line another day. All three Foxboro shows of fifty-five thousand each had sold out in a matter of hours. I called the ticket agency every day to ask when my tickets would be ready. What if they ran out? Or what if our tickets weren't all for the same night? I was told that it was all in the computer, something about how various allocations had to be tallied and that when all the other tickets had been sold, they would be able to give me mine. It sounded very mysterious, not to mention suspicious.

I remember the day when, at last, I picked them up. There was no line or hassle. I merely walked up to the counter, gave the nice man my receipts and money, watched him punch a few entries into the computer, and was handed four beautiful red, white, and blue tickets. I had visions of being stuck way up in the far bleachers, but the seats were way better than I dared hope–right on the field, in the second section from the stage. And on Friday, opening night! All my worries were for nothing. No marathon all night waiting lines. I didn't have to suffer at all. Somehow it didn't seem fair, but I wasn't going to argue.

As to what actually transpired on that glorious day of the concert, I have only the kaleidoscopic mashup of memories that my brain has chosen to store, which get better with each retelling. There were the tailgate parties in the parking lot, for instance, which were really more like one big festival of jubilant Stones fans coming together. Though liquor and joints flowed freely, the crowd was pretty well behaved. Undoubtedly this was mostly due to the fact that most of us were too old to get into a lot of trouble. As Dan and I, recalling our own reckless youth, stepped into the nearby woods to relieve ourselves, a young man barely out of puberty pointed at us and remarked in awe, "Gee, I bet you guys have been to all the concerts!" We just smiled and grimaced through gray beards.

When the time came to enter the stadium, we became one with a wide river of humanity, bobbing in the waves from one checkpoint to another, still half expecting at any moment for someone to stop and tell us that our tickets were no good until, finally, we were ushered through the last gate and allowed to enter that vast arena of our dreams, filled with colored lights and swirling confusion.

As it turned out, Josie and Yvonne bumped into a friend who was an usher, and managed to get themselves seated in the very first section—Row 7!—where, with binoculars, they had fabulous views of Mick's crotch and other Stones anatomy. Dan and I, meanwhile, were left to fend for ourselves in seats that suddenly didn't seem so hot.

As the opening chords of "Start Me Up" announced the Stones' appearance on the stage, everyone on the field immediately jumped to attention and stood up on rickety folding chairs to get a better view of the living dots on the stage, which meant that we were forced to do so as well. For two-and-a-half hours, we stood in that awkward position while the band belted out every possible favorite a Stones fan could ask for.

Even from our relatively decent seats, I could just barely make out their faces. But with the aid of huge video screens mounted at either end of the stage, the combination of dots, living and electronic, helped to create the perfect illusion of being right on top of them. (Of course, if you were lucky enough to be sitting in the seventh row, you didn't need video screens.) I watched those talented multimillionaires' faces for a sign of jadedness or resignation, but there was none. Only the look of surprised joy at being there, doing the stuff they were born to do.

Speaking of joy, I ended up watching Dan as much as I watched the Stones, for in a way I was viewing the band through the joyful effect they were having on my friend's musically gifted eyes and ears. The fact that I did not see or hear every little nuance that Dan caught did not matter. The expression on his face was all I needed. I remember him turning to me throughout the whole concert saying, "I can't believe it." Then the next song would begin to play and all we could say in unison was, "Fuck!"

I also viewed the Stones through the spectacle of fifty-five thousand people, all singing and swaying together, like a great Baptist revival. I too found myself singing and swaying, though I very rarely sing or sway, rubbing shoulders with Dan and the young female celebrant to my right, who offered me a toke from her joint. I politely refused, inadvertently giving her a smug look as if to say, "Who needs drugs?" This from a guy for whom booze and rock 'n' roll had always seemed inseparable. But not now, not while the Stones were playing and my body was pumped high as it's ever been.

For me the peak of the evening came when Mick took an elevator to a platform high atop the weird stage scaffolding, lit up like hell with reddish-orange flames, and began to sing my favorite Stones tune "Sympathy for the Devil." I poked Dan in the ribs and felt myself go—or at least as far as a writer can who is at the same time scrutinizing his own emotional reactions.

There is little left to say of that night, except maybe that I fell madly in love with one of the pair of giant, garish but lovely females inflated during "Honky Tonk Women." Inevitably, I am forced to deal with the casual question repeatedly asked by well-meaning people, just trying to make conversation, who have no idea of how difficult it is for me to answer: "Well, how *were* they?"

I tried to come up with some succinct metaphor to convey what I had experienced. All I could think of was, "They edged out Grand Canyon," and left it at that.

The next night, our little group sat at the bar of Tortilla Flat and plotted our next move. "What do we do now? How do we top that?"

We talked of going to England together, someday, when all the credit cards are paid off. Then we raised our glasses for a toast. "OK, five years from now. But weren't those Stones something? And to think we saw them on their very last tour."

Or maybe not. A short time later, as I watched Keith Richards in an interview on MTV, he made a cryptic remark that caught my attention, something about this being only the start of things. Could it be? It seemed impossible at the time, but the Stones could be the first super rock group to play on into their sixties. I can see it all now–the North American Geriatric Tour. And the four of us will be there.

Postscript. It is now 2018, and I am here to report that much has changed, though we still have the dinosaurs. I should know because I'm one of them. For one thing, I still don't own a smartphone. I still get my music from CDs and FM, and desperately miss MTV. There's only one kind of rock and that's classic rock. I totally agree with Bob Seger: "Today's music ain't got the same soul / I like that old-time rock 'n' roll." And our late dear friends Dan and Yvonne have passed into sacred memory. Rock on, guys!

And speaking of dinosaurs, the Stones still rock the earth. Since the band first formed in 1962, they have performed more than two thousand concerts worldwide. On March 26, 2016, they broke an all-time record and played to 500,000 adoring Cubans in Havana, which in retrospect makes our 1989 Foxboro concert seem more like a high school dance. Now both into their seventies, Mick and Keith show no signs of ever stopping. Forget about the Geriatric Tour. How about the Fibrillator Tour? The Cardiac Arrest Tour?

Not that I follow them anymore. A few years after their Steel Wheels Tour in 1989, I tuned into one of their concerts on MTV, but found it too painful to watch. Not that I didn't enjoy hearing them belt out those beloved tunes again. But something had changed. No longer were they young rockers in the prime of life, but aging performers acting as if they were still the same bad boys of rock. Sure, Mick could still sometimes prance around on the stage like Pan on steroids. But now the tempo was slower, almost mellow, with none of the heightened fever pitch of the old days. The band seemed more like dinosaurs ponderously stalking the primal stage to which they once belonged, living fossils of a bygone era. Hey, I know they can still fill stadiums and make young girls scream. Good for them. But while rock 'n' roll may still beat in an old fuck's heart, it's no longer the same body. Sorry, Mick and Keith, you're not the rockers you once were. Hate to hear myself say it, but rock is a young folk's game. You two don't need to fill big stadiums anymore, just so you can get your adrenaline rush and line your pockets. Get back to your roots and sing the blues. There are plenty of smaller venues where you can tour and simply be yourselves, try out some new stuff, and play all those great tunes you appropriated from black musicians. Hey, look at Buddy Guy at 81. You don't see him trying to be something he's not, but he can still kick ass with the best of them.

Oh, one final thing, Mick. Seems you got all pissed off at Keith for joking in a recent interview with *Wall Street Journal* that you should get a vasectomy, after fathering a child with your girlfriend Melanie Hamrick.

That makes eight kids for you, so far, right? I know he's your friend, but Keith shouldn't have apologized. I totally agree with him. Dinosaurs shouldn't breed. Look what happened in *Jurassic Park*.

SPAWN OF CTHULHU

IT IS WITH THE UTMOST deliberation that I write down this account of the peculiar events that transpired in Providence during the weekend of August 17–19, 1990. Bear in mind that I did not actually *see* any visual horror. And there was nothing to suggest that we were visited by weird beings of loathsome proportions or that the affair, strange though it was, has any supernatural or cosmic significance. But the fact that something weirdly remarkable occurred here cannot be denied.

The matter began, so far as I can tell, with a simple birthday party to honor a Providence native son, Howard Philips Lovecraft, who was born on August 20, 1890. From thence the party grew, however, into the weekend-long H.P. Lovecraft Centennial Conference. Sponsored by Brown University and funded by a grant from the Rhode Island Committee for the Humanities, it was an invitation to

Lovecraft scholars and devotees from around the globe to gather and pay long overdue homage to their man.

While relishing the prospect of this international birthday bash, I was also a bit apprehensive about the kind of crowd it would attract to our fair city. The object of these devotions was, after all, an eccentric practitioner of the weirdest kind of tale imaginable. He had populated our serene city streets with the abominable and decadent creations of his fevered mind, and then left them here to fester and haunt us forever.

What kind of person reads this stuff, or worse, spends an inordinate amount of time writing and speaking about it? I tried to imagine what the participants might be like. Would they be bookworm-y types, with pasty faces and humped shoulders, wearing crumpled, moth-eaten suits? Or would they be spiky-haired, fish-faced cultists, with strange geometric tattoos and bizarre T-shirts? Or perhaps would suddenly descend upon us, a legion of identical dark-eyed gentlemen, wearing flowing Windsor ties and black knee-length capes over wrinkled and ill-kempt clothing?

All right, I too have dipped a little into Lovecraft. It started in my teenage years, that period of life most susceptible to morbid fixations and idle experiments. I discovered him in the local library, in the dusty pages of Arkham House first editions, which later mysteriously vanished. The cosmic monsters for which he is famous—

Cthulhu (pronounced "kuh-THOO-loo"), Dagon, Hastur, Shub-Niggurath, Azathoth,Yog-Sothoth, and the fabulous Fungi from Yuggoth, to name a few–I found curious but not frightening, no more so than ghosts, werewolves, or old Satan himself. Indeed, Lovecraft's creatures are almost laughable. Are we really supposed to be frightened by the wrinkled, pinkish crabs with fungus faces known as the Fungi from Yuggoth? And as for Azathoth, which HPL described as an "amorphous blight of nethermost confusion which blasphemes and bubbles at the center of all infinity," well, it is difficult to get all worked up over a monster that blasphemes and bubbles at the same time.

Rather, I was moved by the author's ability to create settings and moods of horror so convincingly real that even today I cannot drive through the "wild domed hills of Vermont" with their "dark valleys where streams trickle from unknown sources" without smiling shivers of joy. Why should a relatively logical, emotionally stable mind like mine be so unsettled by such phrases as "clustered gambrel roofs" and "silent, sleepy, staring houses in the backwoods?" Why should a grown man, grounded in the natural sciences, find anything out of the ordinary in the Lovecraftian observation that "the trees grew too thickly, and their trunks were too big for any healthy New England wood." The forest just needs a good thinning, that's all. But why does a certain part of me insist on seeing something else there? While I would deny to the grave even the remotest possibility that there lurked in such places anything more tangibly dangerous than a writer's thoughts, I was yet filled with fear and wonder at the strange dark depths of the human psyche that Lovecraft revealed to me.

Admitting all this, I must add that I am more a dilettante than a true devotee of Lovecraft. Other writers touch me where I live more reliably. I tend to snicker too much to sustain in either my reading or writing the heightened level of cosmic fear and trembling that Lovecraft was able to bring to his fiction. These days, I read him only rarely, when a foul and decadent mood descends upon me and I need to be comforted by one who understood.

It was like HPL's story "The Outsider" when I approached the John Hay Library on Friday night, where I knew the inner circle of disciples had gathered. They would probably be assembled in one of the smaller rooms upstairs, I thought, as I groped and stumbled up the stone steps and through the door of the venerable Ivy League castle. Immediately upon entering, however, I was met not by the quiet comforting dimness I had always known but by surroundings "gorgeously ablaze with light and sending forth sound of the gayest revelry." Was this the right place? Where were the scholars, bookworms, and cultists? The few people I saw at first sight, clutching plastic wine glasses and prodigious plates of food, hardly seemed eccentric enough to be Lovecraft fans.

But I was totally unprepared for that which lay ahead in the next room. For there, in the vast expanses of the reading room, thronged a mind-numbing multitude . . . "an oddly dressed company, indeed; making merry, and speaking brightly to one another." And while it is true that "some of the faces seemed to hold expressions that brought up incredibly remote recollections," on the whole they seemed like a fun group.

Though having arrived near the end of the reception, I paused for a few minutes to examine some of the materials from the library's unexcelled Lovecraft collection of letters, manuscripts, and art work. At the sight of his handwritten first drafts, filled with crossed out sentences and marginal notes, I winced and smiled in empathy. What could he have done with a word processor, I wondered. Most likely, he would have been horrified at even the thought of one, as some writers still are today.

Hanging on the walls of one room were various examples of artwork inspired by Lovecraft's stories. There was the poster for that wonderfully terrible movie (starring Sandra Dee) based on "The Dunwich Horror." There was also the garish poster advertising the 1971 Ballantine edition of *The Survivor and Others*, a copy of which once hung proudly in my room at college.

Saturday morning found me at the Brown Salomon Center, ready to absorb whatever I could stomach. More a literary scanner than a scholar, I began to wonder if I had the stamina to sit through this colossal Lovecraftian marathon. In addition to scheduled walking tours and other activities, there were six panel discussions. Each was composed of four or five certified Lovecraft scholars and ran for an hour-and-a-half. Some of the scholars had travelled, at their own expense, from as far away as France, Germany, and Cranston, Rhode Island. I therefore resolved to at least try to avail myself of whatever wisdom they had to offer. And, with the day being hot and sticky, there were worse places to be than in an air-conditioned auditorium.

From my seat in the back corner I watched as the large lecture room filled. Each of the four panels that day were well attended. The crowd was an interesting mixture of bearded long hairs, academics, preppies, and assorted misfit loners. Dress ranged from semiformal to slovenly. Though I saw no flowing black capes, a number of fine T-shirts were in evidence. I particularly liked the "Lovecraft for Mayor" and the sporty "Miskatonic University" (after HPL's fictional university in witch-haunted Arkham). The long-haired young man in the "Helter-Skelter" shirt did give me pause, however.

It was a very white-looking audience, mostly Anglo-Saxon and Nordic, with only a sprinkling of other races and ethnic groups. While one panelist, Harry Beckwith, addressed the topic of HPL's early xenophobia (commenting that Howard didn't have much use for any group other than his own), I found myself wondering if some folks still hold it against the writer that he once described them as "lesser divisions of mankind" or "stinking mongrel vermin." As Beckwith pointed out, Lovecraft was, in many ways, merely a reflection of his times and, indeed, later outgrew such notions. I would be interested to see the racial and ethnic composition of the bicentennial conference.

Somehow, I managed to make it through the other panels, during which scholars discussed in minutest detail every aspect of the author's personal life and writing, including even his medical history and which hospital room he occupied. With maybe one exception, the panelists came not to pontificate but to share their special insights, as well as to listen and learn themselves. While many in the audience attempted to fill their notebooks with every precious morsel, and some even taped the proceedings, at times I found myself zooming in on certain comments, then drifting off to nether regions, until the whole seemed like some surrealistic smorgasbord. Even now, I find myself wondering if it all was but a dream.

What little I do remember of that time probably reveals more about the confused nature of my mind than about what was actually said. Perhaps "the most merciful thing in the world," Lovecraft wrote, "is the inability of the human mind to correlate all its contents." I shall not attempt to do so here except to share a few impressions.

I distinctly remember that all five members of the first panel had facial hair (three beards and two moustaches). Why I should recall this is beyond me. Perhaps the significance of facial hair, or lack thereof, in Lovecraft's fiction is an area that needs more attention.

I think it was Will Murray who spoke of how Lovecraft was attracted to Massachusetts as a "seat of weirdness." Having grown up in next door Connecticut, I can attest to that. But when he started talking about the floating nature of Arkham (Lovecraft's fictional version of Salem, more or less), he lost me.

During the second panel, we listened to Harry Brobst's taped personal reminiscence of HPL. Alas, it was filled with so much background noise that it sounded like it was coming "From Beyond." We did learn about Howard's dust-covered books and dirty bed in his room at 10 Barnes Street, and that during his last year the twinkle went out of his eye.

Eileen McNamara told us that, while Lovecraft most certainly did not have syphilis or suffer from any major mood disorders, he may have had temporal lobe epilepsy, which could explain why he felt compelled to write fifty zillion letters. We also learned that, in the last days of his life, the author was admitted to a room on the second floor of the Jane Brown Hospital, though we don't know exactly which one because all the rooms have been renumbered. The charge was $7 per day.

An unexpected treat was a visit from Frank Belknap Long, biographer and long-time friend of Lovecraft as well as a respected horror story writer himself. With flowing white hair and beard, he reminded me of Gandalf from *Lord of the Rings.* With the aid of a walker, he slowly made his way to the stage. When asked to comment on the supposedly peculiar nature of Howard's voice, Long admitted that it was slightly high-pitched, but thought it a "typical New England voice."

By the third panel, I was beginning to wonder if I would make it through the weekend and was secretly glad that HPL hadn't written more stuff. I do remember the moderator briefly commenting on the Lovecraftian use of long-winded sentences and subjective adjectives—a technique imitated by many neophyte writers, including myself. Referring to that famous story "The Rats in the Walls," he drolly noted: "You'd probably use them too if you had just discovered a vast twilit grotto and the fact that your family were all cannibals . . ."

And then there was John McInnis, who delivered an autobiographical reading of "The Colour Out of Space." It sounded strange though not unpleasant to hear old HPL discussed in a deep Southern drawl. All I remember is something about Lovecraft senior being compared to a meteorite.

Meanwhile, as R. Boerem philosophized on the great threat to humanity implied by this story—to have the very meaning of existence sucked, as it were, right out of our lives by an uncaring universe–I found my attention drifting from the panelists to the audience. For indeed they were the real show. Nodding their heads enthusiastically or sometimes shaking their fists at the speakers, they all seemed to be having a splendid time. I had the feeling that it didn't matter all that much what the panelists said, just as long as it had something to do with HPL. It was as if the panelists had been invited, like ministers, to come say a few words and share the joy of Lovecraft's tales of cosmic horror, as we celebrants basked in the glow of our fellowship.

By this time, I was glad to get outside for what I had hoped would be a nice, leisurely walking tour of some of Lovecraft's haunts. I merged with the crowd assembling around S.T. Joshi, noted HPL scholar and author of a most readable book *The Weird Tale.* Unfortunately, the author walks as briskly as he writes, and I was able to catch only fleeting glimpses of places as we ran by them on our marathon tour. Most of the time, the crowd remained far ahead of me, flowing into the streets and blocking traffic, while occasionally stopping to mass around this or that building.

One of the stops was Lovecraft's last home, which had been moved from its original site, at 66 College Street, to its current location, at 65 Prospect Street. As the crowd shot up the street, I paused to stare at the curtained open window of his second-floor room. I could imagine him sitting there, gazing out over the city while voyaging through "black seas of infinity."

I caught up with the group for a brief moment at 10 Barnes Street, where the author lived after his short marriage and divorce. Here he wrote a number of his most famous stories. Now a privately-owned apartment house, its student occupants insist that they sometimes hear Howard's ghost.

I also stopped by to see the sinister-looking (at least to HPL) Charles Dexter Ward House, at 140 Prospect Street. And of course, the house, at 133 Benefit Street, made famous in the story "The Shunned House." This time, no weird glow emanated from the basement. I imagine whoever lives here must get awfully tired of Lovecraft fans trying to peer inside. Two small signs to the right, however, reading "chien bizarre" and "chien lunatique" filled me with dread.

I caught up with the group one last time at Prospect Terrace, where Lovecraft often spent afternoons reading. This was supposed to be the site for the commemorative plaque purchased by The Friends of H.P. Lovecraft. The site had to be changed, however, to an area just outside the John Hay Library. Apparently, there's a park rule that commemorative plaques can't be named after someone. Sorry, Howard.

At the terrace, I parted company with the tour, or rather, they left me in the dust. Still in the mood, I ambled along Angell Street and logged a few more sites in Lovecraft's Providence: 276 Angell Street, which features as the Archer Harris House in "The Shunned House;" 454, now an empty lot at the corner of Elmgrove Avenue, where the author's birthplace once stood; and 598, where his family moved after the death of his grandfather. (For more information, I highly recommend the book *Lovecraft's Providence & Adjacent Parts* by Henry L. Beckwith.)

On Sunday afternoon, after attending one last panel discussion, I squeezed in amongst a few dozen hard-core fans to witness the unveiling of the commemorative plaque. We listened as Jon Cooke, editor of the *Centennial Guidebook*, referred to all of us gathered here this weekend as friends of the writer, one and all. Then the party slowly dispersed, some to the HPL Film Festival scheduled at 3, but most I suspect to their various homes throughout the country and overseas.

Later, I returned alone to take another look at the plaque. It is simple and tasteful, set within native granite. Under his name are the words "U.S. Author." Not horror story author, just author. I like that. Writers, whatever their genre and despite their differences, are far more alike than not.

I mentioned at the outset that I did not actually see any horrors that weekend. I did see some weird beings, however. In every respect they are the living, breathing spawn of great Cthulhu himself. True, most of them are not exactly how S. Peterson's *Field Guide to Cthulhu Monsters* describes them: "bloated entities with dragon-like wings and talons, and faces covered by barbels." Nevertheless, as "entities of great power, they can travel through space at will, plunging from world to world."

And while it may seem remarkable that a few hundred of them gathered here to perform their nameless rites, there is no cause for alarm or surprise. After all, they were just being human. Like Cthulhu's creator, as panelist David Schultz pointed out, they were preoccupied not so much with monsters as with asking who and what we are.

Lovecraft knew the answer, of course. We are creatures of the written word–readers and writers all. And you can't be more human than that.

Unless otherwise noted, all quoted material is from various Arkham House collections of H.P. Lovecraft's stories, L. Sprague de Camp's biography, *Lovecraft,* and the Wormius edition of the *Necronomicon.*

A PAINLESS GUIDE TO TRAUMA

HUMAN LIFE IS ONE LONG trauma, from the moment you get evicted from your hot tub womb to face the cold glare of an unforgiving world. Then all you hear is, study hard. Stand up straight. Make a lot of money. Marry someone so I can have grandkids. And be happy! Until someday you realize you're just going to die like everyone else and, most likely, you'll be surrounded by people you don't know while you soil yourself on the way out.

But throw some extra trauma into the mix–sexual abuse maybe, severe depression, or Post Traumatic Stress Disorder (PTSD)–and life can seem unendurable. While some people decide they cannot go on living, most of those afflicted manage to deal with it, often in unexpected ways.

If you dig into the life of any famous author, more than likely you'll find at least one or more traumas lurking behind the scenes.

Take my favorite author Kurt Vonnegut. At the onset of World War II, he enlists in the Army, at which his mother is so upset that she commits suicide. He promptly gets captured by the Germans, is locked up in a slaughterhouse in Dresden, where he survives the firebombing only to emerge upon a scene straight out of a Hieronymus Bosch painting and is forced to dig up the burnt remains of humans who once laughed and made love. The war soon ends, and he goes back to the States to get on with life.

But how does one get on with life after that sort of thing? Don't know about you, but I would want to dig a deep bomb shelter, well-stocked of course, with booze, comfort food, and every DVD episode of *Friends, Cheers, Seinfeld,* and *Star Trek,* and numb my brain into oblivion.

Fortunately for those of us who love his books, Vonnegut chose not to retreat. Instead he found a way to channel the shock and horror of what he had experienced into *Slaughterhouse Five,* followed by a series of other humorous dark novels. But he paid a terrible price. The shadow of war's absurdity would haunt him for the rest of his days.

Then there was Sylvia Plath, who made an all too brief writing career out of the depression and despair which colored most of her poems and her novel *The Bell Jar.* In her journals she wrote that "the loneliness of the soul in its appalling self-consciousness is horrible and overpowering." Overpowering enough that she took her life at age thirty.

You probably won't admit it, but haven't you, in darker moments, idly thought about suicide? You're standing on the subway platform and, just as the train pulls in, you catch yourself wondering, "Gee, what if I really did it?" followed by a string of other thoughts. "What would that be like? Boy, I'll bet they'd miss me. Or maybe not. At least I wouldn't have to study for that exam. I just know I'm gonna flunk."

For James Baldwin, grand master of the personal essay, suicide was an ever-present option. In his semi-autobiographical novella *Giovanni's Room*, his character wrote: "I simply wondered about the dead because their days had ended and I did not know how I would get through mine." In real life, he tried killing himself several times, but failed. The fact that his father considered him hideous because of his so-called "frog-eyes" and actually told him that he was "the ugliest boy he had ever seen" probably didn't help. Ya think?

OK, what about J.K. Rowling? How could she *not* be happy and fulfilled with all those gazillions from her Harry Potter books? Yet here she is describing her severe depression as "the absence of hope. That very deadened feeling, which is so very different from feeling sad. Sad hurts but it's a healthy feeling. It is a necessary thing to feel. Depression is very different."

Stephen King's life sounds like one long horror story of fear and dependency. Growing up in poverty, he was traumatized at age two by a philandering father who abandoned his family. His mother was forced to take low-paying jobs and hand him off to be cared for by relatives. He was haunted by the fear that she too would abandon him, leading to constant insecurity and nightmare terrors including his own and his mother's death, falling down toilets, clowns, and *spiders.* He found partial relief through writing stories about these fears, and later through heavy drinking and cocaine use. But with the death of his mother, he sank into a drunken, doped out depression so severe that through much of the '80s he could not remember how he had written the horror novels for which he is best known.

With the help of his wife, Tabitha, King eventually overcame his dependency, but still writes about his fears as a means of therapy. Someday he hopes to be able to write about his worst fear–spiders.

Some recent studies have suggested a possible link between trauma and creativity. One such study, conducted by Marie Forgeard of the University of Pennsylvania and published in *Psychology of Aesthetics, Creativity, and the Arts,* showed a strong connection between the number of traumatic events in a person's life and creative growth.

Admittedly, there are probably many great writers who never suffered a day in their life from trauma, though they escape me at the moment. The closest one I can think of is E.B. White, brilliant essayist and the author of the beloved children's novels *Charlotte's Web* and *Stuart Little.* A lifelong hypochondriac, he did suffer from bouts of minor depression. Yet he managed to escape the raging, drunken depression that plagued his friend and colleague James Thurber.

So, where does this leave a writer like me, seventy years old, with not a single trauma I can think of that has influenced and shaped my writing?

As far as I know, I've never been abused, sexually or otherwise. My wife, Josie, upon reading the graphic scenes of sexual abuse from the first draft of my young adult novel *My Vacation in Hell,* did once ask me, "Are you sure you were never abused?" I took this as a compliment. But then, one never knows. Someday, in my nineties, with the aid of a good therapist, I could discover that I was abused. And Josie will say, "See, I was right."

I did have a high school algebra teacher who gave me a hard time, especially when, as was usually the case, he noticed I had my nose in a science book during class. He would choose me to go to the blackboard as he sneered and said, "See if you can solve *this* problem, Twaronite." Thankfully the nightmares have stopped, though I still hate algebra.

My gym teacher in junior high school was a former Marines drill instructor, who often treated us students as if we were a bunch of new recruits. He would bark out questions to us, and when none of us could answer, had us run or do extra calisthenics. Pity the poor little fat boy who couldn't keep up or climb a rope. He would launch into him unmercifully with a string of colorful insults. Some of the tougher boys, however, would stand up to him in defiance. For their reward, they would be forced to either run laps around the field till they dropped or fight him after school. Reasonably fit, I mostly escaped his wrath, though later, as my physique developed, he would badger me constantly to go out for the football team. "What's the matter, Twaronite? Are you un-American or something?"

Besides teacher bullies, there were the usual bullies in class. The worst one was in elementary school. I was the teacher's pet and always knew the answers. So, he was always in my face asking, "Ya think you're smart, don't you? Well, why won't you fight me, huh?" I don't know whether it was my size or my scintillating comebacks, but he never started anything with me, like shoving me or grabbing my girlfriend, whom I walked home after school each day to protect her from the likes of him. It really bugged him that he couldn't get me to fight. As I think back on it, he displayed a certain intelligence and seemed more of a reluctant bully, as if it were just a job he had to do. Nothing personal. He had a real code of honor, and would not hit someone unless he could somehow provoke him to hit first.

One day, he pushed the envelope a little and said he

wished me to address him with the prefix "Master" added to his name. I think he had just heard it somewhere and it sounded cool. I simply shrugged and, for the next couple of days, obliged him until he forgot.

What about my parents? you say. No luck there, either. Alas, they were both perfectly stable, with a happy marriage that lasted over sixty years. Our family wasn't exactly rich, but we weren't poor. My dad was a mailman, while my mother worked occasionally at a nearby factory, where she sewed parachutes. Not exactly the stuff of Dickens. Worse yet, they actually loved me and thought I was the smartest, handsomest boy on the planet, except for my brother, of course. To the annoyance of relatives and friends, they bragged about us constantly, and never pressured us into becoming anything other than what we wanted to be. They were the best parents a guy could possibly ask for. Damn!

No physical ailments to speak of, either. I was healthy as a horse. And, despite the fact that most of high school was one long emotional trauma because of all the screwups, hang-ups, and people I managed to hurt, there did not seem to be any lasting psychic damage.

During my senior year at college, however, I discovered drinking in a big way. This was largely the result of two things. I had commuted from home the first three years, and was about as socially isolated and deprived as a lone hermit crab in an aquarium. And as a devout Catholic, I actually took a Confirmation pledge not to drink until age twenty-one. Does anyone still do that?

So, when I arrived at that magical age and finally made it to campus, populated by numerous lovely female students, it all hit me like a tsunami. I would go to so-called mixers where, with the aid of keg beer, you were supposed to dance and mingle. Hard to believe, but I was painfully shy in those days and had not yet learned that the real secret of dancing is not to give a shit about what anyone thinks of you on the dance floor. I would drink myself stupid trying to summon up courage to dance, which I never did. As for lovemaking, it was pretty much a disaster, since I always insisted on getting drunk first. I somehow managed to graduate with high honors, though don't ask me how I did it.

The heavy drinking continued into my twenties and thirties. I'm not proud to admit it, but sometimes I would get behind the wheel and drive. Once again, dumb luck saved me from disaster. Killing myself was one thing. I could live with that. Killing someone else was entirely different. It could have been my first trauma.

I could have also gone the way of several uncles on my mother's side, both navy veterans of WW II, who lost the battle with booze. I could have developed into a full-blown alcoholic. Who knows what great writing it would have inspired, as I daily grappled with my demons? But by middle age, getting shit-faced every time I drank had gradually lost its appeal, while my body was no longer willing to endure next morning's aftermath. Several times, I had even tried to write while drunk, as some of my writer heroes had purportedly done. I am here to report that the resulting gibberish left me unimpressed.

Though, technically, I am still a moderate to heavy drinker, consuming my daily ration of two or three beers and wines, I never went down the rabbit hole. It remains to be seen how my liver and other organs will fare.

I also escaped the trauma of PTSD, since I never served in the military, or played football, for that matter. While the Vietnam War raged, I was attending college and getting good grades, so I was temporarily exempt from the draft. Until December of 1969, that is. That was when the U.S. Selective Service System instituted the lottery, for men born from 1944–1950. Based on the number of days in the year, it would determine who would be called up next, college or no college. I remember all of us guys sitting in the dormitory anxiously listening and drinking as the numbers were called out. Some guy in the back would moan as he heard his name and the unlucky number 7 or 11. My number ended up in the low 200s. If my birthday had been one day earlier, my draft number would have been called for sure. My lifelong friend from kindergarten, born only a few days later, ended up home free in the 360s. I was of course happy for him, the lucky bastard.

As things turned out, they never called up past

number 195, but it was still way too close for me. In those days, I was largely apolitical, though I had read enough to know that the Vietnam War was immoral, unwinnable, and just plain stupid, and the mere thought of being drafted filled me with horror. So much so that on the day I was called to report for my physical, my body reeled in existential angst. During the train ride down to New Haven, all I could think of was having to crawl through some rice paddy while bullets sailed past my helmet. When I got there, it was surreal, straight out of the movie scene from *Alice's Restaurant*, though without the Group W bench. When I was finally examined, the doctor took my pulse and it read 140. "What are you on?" he asked, in a most sarcastic tone. I assured him that I was drug free, but he insisted on keeping me in the exam room for hours and hours. But 140 it remained, until late in the afternoon, when the doctors shook their heads and released me to take the last train home, along with a written order to have my pulse taken for three consecutive days.

Dutifully, each day, I ran to the infirmary, after drinking copious amounts of coffee–no sense taking chances–where my pulse remained near 120 for three days. High enough so that I was eventually classified by my local draft board as 1-H, which meant that I was "not currently subject to processing for induction or alternative service," though I suspect that if things got really bad, I could still be called up, high pulse rate or not.

Watching all ten episodes of the Ken Burns documentary on the Vietnam War was as close as I ever got to what happened there. The film forced me to confront the war's tragic aftermath and the complicated stories of men who volunteered and served there honorably, only to be spit upon and called baby killers upon their return. Some served just as honorably by actively protesting the war, or becoming medics or conscientious objectors. Others chose Canada. I never had to face that choice, and it still haunts me today. I was given a free pass and I gladly took it.

The closest I came to a real trauma involved rejecting religion. Throughout my college years right up into my early twenties, I took the Catholic faith in which I had been raised seriously–I mean, really seriously–so much so that at one point I considered a vocation as a Franciscan brother. Never a priest, however. Too much chanting, drama, and ritual. I just couldn't see myself up there on the altar performing my sacred duties in the spotlight. And those vestments seemed too much like dresses, reminding me of the minor trauma suffered in sixth grade, when I had to don a dress for a lead in a humorous play shown in front of the entire school. I preferred to be a brother, quietly performing some humble task in the background for the glory of God.

For a brief time, I thought I had found the perfect

answer to life. If the God of my Catholic faith really existed, then to risk an eternity in heaven for the brief pleasures of a mortal life would be folly. Why not go for the sure thing? The idea of a simple monastic life fully given to God was one I devoutly wished to believe in—I also liked the robe. It would make choosing what to do with my life so much easier.

But the central question remained: *if this be true.* For years, I read and studied deeply the tenets of my own faith while also taking courses in philosophy and comparative religion. After considerable internal debate and reflection, I found all the arguments used to support Catholicism, and other religions as well, thoroughly unconvincing. For me to embrace their extraordinary claims would require that I renounce my rational side and simply accept them based on nothing more than conflicting, anecdotal accounts of miracles and events I know can't possibly be true. It was a wrenching personal struggle, but in the end, I came out stronger and better able to understand myself. I had left the comforting belief system that had sustained me from my earliest years. But I had gained a new, more open way of looking at the world unchained by dogma or preconception. And I have learned, after many years, to simply smile and not get angry when someone stops me on the corner and presumes to ask, "have you heard the 'Good News'?"

Meanwhile, I'll just have to play out the trauma-less

life I've been given, writing about all its little dramas, waiting for the inevitable blow. Not that I'm looking forward to it. Take your time, I say. No rush. But one thing I know. You don't get out of here without at least one trauma. I guess there's hope for me yet.

HOW I MET VONNEGUT OR GOODBYE, BLUE MONDAY!

BACK WHEN I LIVED IN Providence in November 1990, a short, offhand blurb on page four of the local paper (for which I wrote) quietly announced that Kurt Vonnegut would be in town to address Brown University students at Alumnae Hall. "Check to see if any tickets remain," said the article.

Say what?!

In exactly twenty-four hours, one of the major writers of the twentieth century and my all-time hero was scheduled to appear at my very door. My chances of getting a ticket now were about as slim as finding a rent-controlled apartment in Trump Tower. Nonetheless, I ran like a bad rumor over to Brown–only to be told that all 600 tickets had been handed out a week ago, two tickets per Brown ID. It was shaping up to be a blue Monday, indeed.

"Why don't you just go over there and tell them you

write for a local newspaper?" asked my wife in a cheery, optimistic voice. "There's your ticket."

Raising my head slowly out of a bowl of soggy corn flakes in which I was trying to drown myself, I looked at her and laughed. "Yeah, right. With hundreds of bigwig journalists there, from George Wills and Mark Patinkin to Hunter Thompson and, who knows, maybe Tom Wolfe, do you really think they're going to let me in there? Don't be absurd."

"Got any better ideas?" asked Josie, in her gentle tone of why-did-I-marry-this-jerk sarcasm.

I did not. But I called the Brown News Bureau and introduced myself. "Hello, my name is Gene Twaronite and I write for The East Side Monthly. I've been assigned to write an article on the Vonnegut lecture. I was wondering if–"

"Who did you say you are?" asked the young woman. "Isn't that the paper that runs all those disgusting sex ads?"

"No, that's the other paper," I reassured her. "We only run ads for poodles and politicians."

"A press conference has been scheduled for three," she said. "Just show your press card at the door. There will also be a section reserved for the media at tonight's lecture."

"I don't have a press card. My publisher says they're too expensive."

"Are you sure you're a writer?" she asked, like I was

something from the bottom of a dumpster.

After a short enumeration of my writing credits and the promise that I would throw myself off the Point Street Bridge if I didn't get to see Vonnegut, she reluctantly agreed to meet me later at the door. I will remember her kindness always.

Shortly before three, I was allowed to enter and ushered into the inner sanctum–a small side room of the Maddock Alumni Center. Furtively I looked around, still expecting someone to challenge my credentials. But the expected horde of media hounds had so far failed to materialize. There wasn't even a podium or microphone in sight. Just a few dozen folding chairs set in front of an overstuffed pink chair in a corner near the window.

Journalists started trickling into the room, though none of them were from the NY Times or Newsweek. There were eighteen of us in all, many from student newspapers. Tom Wolfe was nowhere to be seen.

Expecting to get no closer than five hundred feet, I had brought with me a 300 mm telephoto lens for my camera, which I hoped would also certify me as a bona fide journalist. I had also equipped myself with a crisp new first edition of Vonnegut's latest novel Hocus Pocus. One never knows.

Suddenly, he appeared. Wearing a dark grey suit, tie, and V-neck sweater, he strode gracefully into the room like a wise, beloved professor and quietly took his seat. Then, as if addressing old friends, he began to talk in a soft, reassuring voice.

"I'll be speaking six times this year, speaking in some strange places . . . though this isn't one of them."

Then he launched into his opening remarks about the deplorable state of the country today and how "we are miserably led." As he warmed to his subject, the pace and intensity of his words picked up. He described the choice of Dan Quayle for vice-president as "a terrible insult to the American people." Sitting back and crossing his legs, he reminded me of a less flamboyant Mark Twain. His hollow, slightly vacant eyes—eyes that had seen too much yet never enough of this crazy world—stared back at us with a mixture of mirth and madness, inviting us to join the party. "Life is fooling around."

With the precise timing of a good comic, he fired off one extravagant remark after another, occasionally interspersing them with common sense observations revealing the intense humanism that fueled his cynicism.

"I can understand people wanting to be doctors or lawyers or teachers. But people who want to be managers, well . . . something is wrong with them."

"Government's a TV show."

"The ideal government is an extended family."

"I took my junior civics course in grade school quite seriously."

Asked by Providence Journal-Bulletin reporter Bob Kerr if "there is anyone you find particularly hopeful," Vonnegut replied without hesitation. "Yes, the American people."

Swallowing hard, I finally summoned the courage to ask my own question. "In your novel Galapagos, you raised the point that our brains may be too big for our own good. Do you–"

He cut me off, delighted to be given this tangent, and went on to compare our brains to the ridiculously over-sized antlers of the extinct Irish elk. "Nature may have made a mistake."

For a few more minutes, Vonnegut bantered with the media. He came to lecture, he told us, usually at the invitation of students, not faculty. He doubted if anyone from the English Department would be in attendance that night. To hear him tell it, he was a virtual nobody in the academic world. (This despite the fact that a seminar on his works was held by the Modern Language Association at its annual international convention back in 1975, where he was compared to such world class authors as Nabokov, Swift, and Twain. It was not the first or the last of such seminars).

Lost in sad reverie over one of his parting comments that "there were a lot of swell writers in the world who just weren't ever going to be noticed," I was caught by surprise when suddenly the author bolted out of his chair and began heading for the door. I remembered the book in my knapsack and lunged to intercept him.

He was almost home free, but I nabbed him just in time. "Mr. Vonnegut," I asked in a timid voice. "This may seem tacky, but ... would you mind signing my book?"

"Not at all," he replied, staring at me with those wild, wonderful eyes of his. Then on the endpaper he made his famous scribble, complete with a certain orifice that some people mistake for a star.

That evening, having been told that press seats would be limited, I arrived at Alumnae Hall forty-five minutes early. I needn't have worried. The first three rows on the left had been reserved for me and my fellow journalists. Being the first one there, I sat down in my privileged seat as the hall quickly filled to capacity and overflowed to the balcony and much of the floor.

Actually, the best seats in the house were reserved for the creative writing class. And sitting among the students, as if to nullify the author's earlier prediction, were some unmistakably professorial types.

I was especially interested in hearing what Vonnegut had to say about how to be a writer. This time, there was a podium and even a blackboard. Right on time, he stepped up to the microphone and began to address the crowd with the same unpretentious grace as that afternoon.

He introduced himself as having been born of the last generation of novelists "whose brains were marinated in books." He then told us that, if as some people claim, rock 'n' roll can cause suicides, he did not want anyone to read his latest book.

Commenting on the Voyager Spacecraft's trip past the Outer Planets, the author displayed his scientific bias, proclaiming this "the most beautiful thing humans have ever done. Just think of it–we made that thing!"

For a while, he read animatedly from a prepared speech, which emphasized the darker side of his worldview. "We are swamped with bad news," he reminded us, then ran through a checklist of his most deeply felt social and environmental issues, as if making sure we all knew he wasn't just some flaky novelist.

He even slipped in a quick lesson on transcendental meditation, describing this state as like "scuba diving in warm bouillon." Then he compared it to reading–"the meditative state of Western Society."

Finally, he got around to the topic I'd been waiting for, though I really didn't expect he'd have much to say. In his diverse collection of essays and stories, Wampeters, Foma & Grandfalloons, he wrote that "you can't teach people to write well. Writing well is something God lets you do or declines to let you do. (This from an avowed atheist.)

He told us there are two main ways to support yourself as a writer: inherit money, or marry a rich person.

He then gave us one of his cardinal rules of revision–throw away the first three pages of any manuscript. It's just needless introductory clutter.

Stepping to the blackboard, he began to draw graphs illustrating the curvature of various kinds of stories. He was always trying to bring much-needed science to English departments.

At the end of his lecture, commenting on the changing nature of student questions these days, he recalled that back when he was a young man on campus, when the world seemed to be in flames and Europe and Asia were on the verge of being swallowed up by Hitler, the burning question was: "Does penis size really matter?"

Whereas now the question he is asked most frequently is: "Do you use a word processor?" I detected a note of sadness in his voice.

So it goes.

A WINTER VISITOR

A RECENT DEATH IN MY family brought me back East, and I took the occasion of revisiting Walden Pond in Concord, the site of Henry David Thoreau's famous experiment in living. After finding solace in a walk around the pond's surprisingly still clear waters, I toured a replica of Thoreau's tiny 10-foot by 15-foot cabin, which he built himself and occupied for twenty-six months from 1845–1847. This was no shack in the woods. It was a sturdy structure, elegant in its simplicity, with a shingled roof and siding, plastered walls, two large windows, a cozy brick fireplace, a closet and a garret with two trap doors.

I tried to imagine him sitting there on a warm summer evening, with the door wide open to catch the breeze. Visibly lacking was an entertainment center or country kitchen with island counters. There was just enough room for his bed, table, cook stove, writing desk and the three chairs Thoreau deemed sufficient ("one for solitude, two for friendship, three for society.")

I found myself wondering what Thoreau might have thought about our own little cabin. Though less ascetically inclined than Thoreau, my wife Josie and I still shared his basic philosophy. We wished to live simply and efficiently in a small house, set in a natural landscape where we could pursue our own experiments in living, one of which involved adjusting to our recent semi-retired, fixed income status. While envisioning something closer to the size of Thoreau's cabin, I did have to concede to Josie that indoor plumbing and a bathroom would be nice as well as a couple of extra rooms for both privacy and company.

Not being able to find any small homes that met our needs, we ended up moving west and purchasing a five-acre lot of pinyon-juniper woodland near Chino Valley, Arizona. Because we wanted something a little more elaborate than Thoreau's cabin and possessed neither the wish nor the skills to tackle the construction ourselves, we hired an architect to develop a plan from the simple drawing Josie had made. After much searching, we managed to locate and hire a local builder to construct the impossible: a custom-built cabin for under $100 per square foot. Fortunately for us, he was between projects, and I think he took the job partly as a challenge to see if he could do it.

Since our goal was a house that intruded as little as possible into our beautiful landscape, our plan called for a building about 25 by 30 feet, with a prow extending another four feet. This would give us a total footprint of 810 square feet. With a peak of 21 feet, we would have room not only for eight large windows on the south side, but also for an upstairs loft accessed by ladder, which gave us a bonus of 320 square feet. Adding this "footprint in the sky," our total area would be 1,130 square feet, or about 7.5 times larger than Thoreau's cabin.

Our plan incorporated a direct gain passive solar design, which is basically using south-facing windows to allow the sun's low-angled rays to enter the house where they are absorbed by interior surfaces and then converted to heat. At least that's what the books said. Lacking any technical training, Josie and I were both still confident that such a design would readily provide most of our heating needs, especially in this little Arizona town that advertises a mild climate and 300 days of annual sunshine. The concept seemed simple, but it is important that there be enough thermal mass in the house's interior to absorb these rays and that some way is found to trap this heat inside (as well as to keep out unwanted heat in the summer). For the thermal mass we decided to use the four-inch thick concrete slab as our uncovered floor. When tinted, sealed and waxed, it gave us an attractive, rustic, and easy to clean surface that would absorb the sun's rays all day and then slowly release the heat at night. The interior of the slab was also insulated from the stem wall with two-inch dense foam, which helps to minimize heat loss into the ground.

The plan called for eight windows on the south side, six 4x6 feet and two 3x4 feet, all dual glazed insulated, with low-E glass. On a bright sunny day, which was most of the time, we found these windows capable of allowing more than an adequate amount of the sun's low-angled rays to enter, and if not for the thermal mass provided by the concrete floor, they would have overheated the house uncomfortably. Aside from a sliding patio glass door on the west side, glazing in the remaining walls was minimal, consisting of five small, double-hung windows, which provided just enough light and ventilation. To trap all this heat, exterior walls were 2x6 feet, with R 22 blown in insulation, which together with the one-inch dense foam beneath the exterior siding brought the walls closer to R 30. R 38 fiberglass insulation was installed in the ceiling. In addition, all windows were fitted with custom, insulated window blinds, which would not only help to keep the heat inside but, as we soon found out, keep it outside in the summer.

Instead of Thoreau's wood shingles, we chose metal roofing, a much longer lasting and far safer alternative in wildfire country; gutters and downspouts were added to allow for directing and harvesting rainwater. For the exterior, we chose a stained texture 1-11 siding, which gave us an economical board and batten look. In place of Thoreau's plastered walls, interiors were rounded sheetrock throughout.

We decided that no central heating or cooling would be required–or so we hoped. Our only backup to the sun was a 36" sealed unit propane fireplace, whose carbon-belching qualities we rationalized by its planned infrequent use and considerable convenience over wood.

While agreeing at least in principle with Thoreau that "many of the so-called comforts of life are not only not indispensable, but positive hindrances to the elevation of mankind," we failed to see how opting for indoor plumbing and a few modern amenities would significantly impede our advancement as human beings. The bathroom, though pretty basic, included a fiberglass tub/shower and cultured marble vanity. Our meager appliance budget allowed us a propane range, dishwasher, electric clothes washer and propane clothes dryer, all Energy Star-rated or as energy-efficient as we could afford. "Incidentals" (which Thoreau undoubtedly would have found inexcusable) also called for fiberglass doors with polished brass levers, oak modular recessed panel cabinets, Formica rolled edge countertops, and 45 square feet of cultured rockwork around the fireplace.

I mention these things merely to demonstrate that our house, though simple and relatively inexpensive to build, still contained many of the conveniences and little touches that many of us today, unlike Thoreau, find indispensable. Of course, his house ended up costing him only $28 and some loose change, or about 19 cents per square foot, not counting his labor. Our house, by comparison, ended up costing $94,313.00, or $83.46 per square foot. When adjusted for 1845 dollars using the Consumer Price Index inflation calculator at one website, this cost becomes $3,794.49, or $3.03 per square foot. Admittedly, this is still a lot more than 19 cents, but then we ended up with the few extras we wanted and construction did not require any labor on our part. One should also note here that Thoreau built his cabin on a woodlot owned by his friend Emerson and could obtain all the potable water he needed from Walden Pond, so I will not include here the costs of our land or well.

Though not as minimal as Thoreau's, our energy needs were still quite modest. The sun met most of our heating needs. To occasionally run our propane fireplace along with a gas clothes dryer, range, and small water heater required about 375 gallons of propane a year. Our monthly electric usage ranged from a low of about 136 kilowatt-hours to a high of about 300 kilowatt-hours in the summer, far below the average monthly usage in the United States of 917 kilowatt-hours. True, our natural house does require of us a more active involvement than a mere flip of the switch. In the winter, windows must be opened and closed, shades pulled and drawn up at strategic times each day, to maximize solar gain. In the summer, after sunset, all windows had to be opened to the cool night air–which at the 4,900-foot altitude usually goes down to the 60s, even in July–then promptly closed in the morning, with all shades drawn, to lock in the coolness and minimize solar gain. Our dim cool cave remains quite comfortable, usually well into the afternoon.

We quickly discovered, however, that on the hottest days, when temperatures often exceeded 100 degrees F., interior temperatures would surpass the low 80s, testing even a desert lover's tolerance. The recent addition of a small ductless, mini-split air conditioner readily keeps the house from overheating during the summer and has proven essential in this era of increasingly higher summer temperatures.

During the four years we lived there, our little house performed better than we dared hope and pleased us more than the lavish monoliths that so many of our generation find desirable. True, we could have built the house for considerably less by learning new skills and doing more of the work ourselves. Instead, we chose a middle path between lavish convenience and stark simplicity. The result is a small but comfortable, moderately priced, energy-efficient home. If he could be here now, what would Thoreau have to say . . . ?

One winter day, a visitor saunters up the pathway leading to our house. The first thing he notices is its size. While larger than his cabin at Walden, our house is considerably smaller than any in the neighborhood as well as those of his previous neighbors in Concord. We invite him in. Upon entering, he takes one look, then shakes his head and says, "Too many chairs. And pray tell, what are all these other things?" with a sweep of his hand and a distinct hint of disapproval in his voice.

"Welcome, Mr. Thoreau. Yes, we probably do have too much stuff, especially compared to your little house. I offer him a chair next to one of the south-facing windows, so he can bask in the warmth of the late December sun and catch a flash of blue as a scrub jay lands in a nearby juniper tree. "What is that bird?" he asks. Then he turns to our fireplace. "I don't see a flame. Tell me, good sir, where does your heat come from on such a cold winter day?"

"From right there," I tell him, pointing through one of the big south-facing windows. "Would you like some tea, Mr. Thoreau? Let me show you our house."

IMPOLITE CONVERSATIONS

IT SEEMS THAT WHENEVER we set out on a family visit, my wife, Josie, takes me aside and reminds me about not discussing certain topics. "What good does it do?" she'll say. "You can't change people's opinions. You'll just get all hot under the collar. Just relax and be sociable."

"What should I talk about?"

"You know! No politics, religion, environment, or health stuff."

"Can I at least talk about philosophy or economics?"

"Hell no. You start talking about the meaning of life and the nature of good and evil, and people get uncomfortable. And you know where any talk about economics will lead. It's capitalism versus socialism, the 1% and the 99%. You want to start a war?"

The only things left are sports and TV, and even those can lead to trouble. "What's with their left baseman? He's got dreads down to his knees. And their catcher's wearing a prayer shawl and a yarmulke. What are you, some kind of bigot? Speaking of bigots, did you see the Donald last night? Man, what a buffoon! Hey, don't knock Donald. He makes a lot of sense. I don't see you making billions of dollars."

You can always talk about the weather. "Say, wasn't that some storm last night? My house is underwater, and they say all of Florida will be soon. Well, at least it put out the wildfires. Do you think all these things have anything to do with...? Don't say it! Say what? You were going to bring up climate change, weren't you? Actually, I was going to say that it might signal the apocalypse, as revealed in Revelations."

Maybe I'm being nostalgic, but wasn't there a time when we could simply talk about things without risking the total meltdown of civilization? Today, there is no real desire to listen and consider anyone else's opinion but one's own. We launch our talking points like missiles, hoping to score points. "Oh, that was a good one. She got you there." Instead of trying to digest what people say, we're too busy thinking about our next clever retort. We ask questions only to embarrass or put off guard anyone who dares to challenge our cherished beliefs. We push our opponents' buttons and laugh as they get flustered.

Have to admit, I'm not always a polite conversationalist. I grow impatient with small talk. I want to suck the marrow out of you, to know what it is you think and feel down to your bones. As far as I'm concerned, the only topics worth talking about are those which inspire, ignite, or anger us, which may explain why I don't receive a lot of dinner invitations.

I miss some of the family dinner discussions we had growing up. Not that they were always civil. I do recall a lot of yelling, but no hitting, biting, or scratching. There would be something in the news about some politician, labor strike, or cultural fad, and we were off. The conversation might veer toward diets, as for instance the time my younger sister became a vegetarian. I remember pummeling her with questions. "What's the matter with meat? Eating meat is natural. What are those canines for, if not to tear flesh? You have to kill something. How is killing a carrot more ethical than killing a cow?" There was much laughter around the dinner table, at my poor sister's expense. As I look back on it, though, beneath the sarcastic veneer, there was a desire to know and understand her reasons. She must have got through to me. It was not long before I, too, became a vegetarian.

Our family was fortunate to have an official discussion referee. Whenever things got too hot in the dining room, my mother, holding a plate of steaming pot roast, would enter and give us all that look. In a grim voice, she would say, "Nutilk!"–the Lithuanian word for "shut up." Then she would smile and tell us to eat.

In her quiet, no nonsense way, my mother was telling us that we were still a family and to put away our differences. For her, *la famiglia* always came first. She saw the dangers of a divided house. Our country is not a family, of course, but as citizens we do, or should, all share a common allegiance to our nation–a nation of many voices, voices that have become increasingly shrill and unyielding. There comes a time when we need to stop shouting at each other and listen for a change. Sit down and break bread. Raise a glass of wine as you toast your differences. And remember to laugh. In the immortal words of both Lincoln and Jesus, "A house divided against itself cannot stand."

INTIMACY AND DENTAL FLOSS

UNTIL YOU TAKE A BAD FALL, you don't know how good life can be when all limbs work properly and you're not dependent upon someone to wipe your ass.

When my life partner Josie took a freak fall one evening while walking home from dinner, the words from our marriage vow "for better or worse" took on a whole new meaning. One moment, she was fine, the next she was flat on her face in the street. Fortunately, having broken the fall with both arms, she had escaped with only a few bruises to her face and her head uninjured. *Unfortunately*, she had managed to completely shatter her right elbow and break her left wrist. As the doctor in the emergency room described the extent of her injuries, I tried to stay calm as I processed the information internally, weighing each word. I could see the neurons flashing a fortune cookie message in my brain: Your life will be filled with new adventures.

Whenever I heard about such stuff happening to

other people, I would try to imagine how I might deal with it. Would I be up to the task when, these days, getting out of bed is challenging enough? I mean, how does one deal with your spouse developing Alzheimer's? Or terminal cancer? Would I be able to face the fact that I was now a 24-7 caregiver for an indeterminate future stretching into a life unknown? What if I ended up having to do everything for my spouse and, like most of us, couldn't afford to pay someone to do it? My mind reeled with the daily realities. Dressing. Feeding. Bathing. Hair brushing and tooth brushing. Walking, including to and from the bathroom, followed by ass wiping. That last part gave me pause. I have enough problems wiping my own ass, but to think I might have to do this for my spouse and also have to deal with how she might feel about it was not something I wanted to think about.

Our situation was only temporary, but I knew that, for months ahead, the carefree retired life we had enjoyed was about to go on hold.

Luckily for me, Josie's mind was still sharp as ever. It meant that I would not have to face this test alone. More than ever, we were a team, devising new strategies to meet daily challenges. Of course, with both arms incapacitated, she was forced to play a more passive role and could only advise me on what to do, gently informing me when I screwed up, and cheering me on when I got it right.

First, we had to establish a base camp for sleeping. We live in a townhouse apartment, and going up and down the stairs to our bedroom was just not an option. Fortunately, we have a guest bedroom with two single beds on the first floor. This meant that Josie could have her own bed without the danger of my rolling over and crushing her arms during the night. Also, I could be in the same room to help her to the adjoining bathroom.

Having secured safe sleeping quarters, I began to reevaluate all those little daily tasks I perform automatically for myself and to consider how best to perform them for another person. Take bathing, for example. You just jump in the shower and start cleaning yourself without so much as a game plan. You don't think about the most efficient way to apply the soap and rinse, or whether you are getting yourself clean enough. But it's different when you're cleaning someone else, especially someone who's wearing bandages that can't get wet. The problem was resolved with a trip to the drugstore where I purchased plastic sleeves to fit over each arm, and a sturdy bathtub seat. Then it was on to Lowe's to pick up a handy shower attachment so I didn't end up flooding the bathroom every time I bathed Josie. But it took us both several weeks of splashing, thrashing, and cursing to figure these things out.

Eating was fun. Not only was Josie totally unable to pick up a fork, but she was still suffering from a recent flareup of orofacial nerve pain as a result of a botched root canal procedure a few years back, and her fall did not exactly help matters. So, we took it slow. I would cut up her meal into bite-size portions and wait until the pain subsided enough for her to eat. We had always enjoyed our dinners together, enlivened by wine and intelligent conversation, but it was painful to watch her struggle now to get a bite down, made even more so by the look on her face from the realization that I had to feed her like an infant. Meals took twice as long. We eventually worked out a routine in which I would alternately feed her a few bites, then take a few bites myself. After a while, she started experimenting with two unbandaged fingers on one hand, and was soon able to pick up small pieces of food herself, though she still could not pick up anything as heavy as a glass in order to drink. Thank goodness for straws.

Funny how you adjust to things and find new insights. After the first week or so, as we settled into a new reality, we started enjoying our much-extended dinner times. No longer would she have to remind me not to wolf my meal. We learned to savor each bite and our time together, made more precious by the knowledge that we had survived this setback and were both still alive and kicking. And if takes us an hour and a half to eat our dinner, hey, so what?

We're both very active people, and Josie knew she had to get moving again. The first few days, she would take walks around the first floor of our apartment, with her trusty guide at her side. The fear of falling was very much on our minds. We were still the same people who had fearlessly tackled rugged trails in the wilderness together. But now that one of us had taken a bad fall, it reminded us how vulnerable our increasingly brittle and fragile bodies can be. I hate that! And I hate writing that line. Reality sucks.

Before leaving the hospital, the physical therapist had given us a broad nylon belt, which could be buckled around Josie's waist while leaving just enough room for my hand to be slipped behind it, giving me a way to hold her firmly in the event of another fall. Such a simple thing, yet an invaluable tool in getting us walking again and conquering our fears. It was a little awkward getting used to, at first, but with me holding on tightly behind her it gave me a way to get us safely down the concrete stairs leading to our apartment and to resume our walks in the neighborhood.

It did feel kind of weird. With my hand planted behind her back and both her arms extended uselessly forward, I felt in complete control, directing her every movement. By turning my hand ever so slightly and applying gentle pressure, I found I could make her turn in the direction I thought we should go to avoid obstacles or rough surfaces as we attempted to walk in unison with some degree of dignity. It was a totally different kind of walking for both of us, and for a brief time I was in charge, whether I liked it or not.

Our walks extended further afield in the neighborhood as we gained confidence. Walking had always been a vital part of our life and now, more than ever, it was essential to get back into the routine.

One thing I noticed. I seemed to tire more quickly. At first, I thought it was just stress. After a couple of weeks had passed and I was able to leave Josie alone for a short time to visit the nearby gym, the normally ten-minute walk now took twice as long and I had to cut my workout sessions short. I always came home exhausted. What was happening to me? Suddenly I felt ninety years old. Then it dawned on me. The older you get, the more time you must devote to the seemingly endless series of routine tasks just to care for oneself each day. Only now, I was doing them for two. Not only did I have to put on clean underwear, but I had to put hers on as well. I had to go to the bathroom, and take her there next, followed by grooming, feeding, drinking, toothbrushing, walking, and whatever else I did for myself. A tiny epiphany, but it gave me both a sense of relief that I was not facing total decrepitude, and a sense of awe at the work that full-time caregivers do.

Not that there weren't compensations. After a few weeks had passed, we settled into a manageable and at times even pleasant routine. We took each day at a slower pace, trying to find some new insight or small pleasure we had overlooked. I began to see things I had never noticed before. As I tried my best to comb Josie's hair, according to her instructions, I felt hopelessly lost at first. It dawned on me, then, that I really didn't have a clue as to how my life partner of over forty years wore her hair, except for the fact that it was short. How she combed her front bangs down slightly to cover her high forehead. How she brushed the hair behind her ears and shaped the back into a point. Had it not been for her fall, I would never have known these things. After a while, I got pretty good with the hairdryer. I imagined myself as some handsome and suave hairdresser–just call me Ramone–getting her hair to fluff up just right. My flight of fancy lasted but two weeks, at which point she decided she could manage her hair without me. Guess I wasn't really cut out for hairdressing.

Bathing presented even more opportunities for new insights and intimacies. Once the basic problem of how to get Josie's body clean efficiently without stressing us both out and flooding the bathroom floor was solved, we gradually settled into a smooth rhythm. I now knew the drill and could devote myself more fully to the appreciation of my spouse's lovely body. Not that I hadn't appreciated it before. But this was different. I was performing a necessary basic task which I had initially viewed as somewhat onerous, but it had taken on a wholly new dimension. Like that first time we had made love, I was clumsy in the beginning, but as my hand glided over her body with a soapy washcloth, I began to see and discover it anew. You do not really know your lover's body until you have washed every inch of her and gently patted her dry. It was a different kind of sexual pleasure, an arousal more of spirit than of body. We both grew to enjoy this gentle touching, as I explored parts of her body never really noticed before in simple lovemaking. And while I am glad that I don't have to wash her anymore, I will remember it always.

Wiping my lover's ass, however, is hardly a memory to cherish. Damned if I could find any compensations there. The only thing I can say looking back on it now is that it wasn't nearly as unpleasant as I had imagined, aided considerably by the use of latex gloves, but largely by the fact that my spouse has a cute ass. But don't take my word for it. During our first year of marriage, I found I needed a new dentist. I made an appointment with Josie's dentist, who I was quick to discover was a lecherous old man with a wicked sense of humor. As I sat agape in his chair, his instruments probing my teeth, out of nowhere he suddenly exclaimed, "You know, your wife has a *great* ass!" I almost choked, as I mumbled some unintelligible reply, then reluctantly nodded. How could I disagree? I had always especially treasured that part of her anatomy. But now that I had to keep it clean each day, I learned to approach the task as a sacred honored duty. It couldn't have been a pleasant experience for her, but once again Josie came through with calm, clear instructions on what needed to be done and where, and got me through it. Hard to believe that such a simple basic thing as wiping my lover's ass could bring us closer and make me feel more needed and more worthy than ever.

But for real intimacy, nothing beats dental hygiene. I thought I knew all the hidden mysteries and intricacies of Josie's body, after all these years, but I still knew nothing of the world inside her mouth. Now Josie is a real stickler for proper brushing, flossing, and rinsing, dutifully spending over half an hour each night in front of the mirror while cursing its relentless monotony. And here I was, stepping up to the plate, in hopes of performing this duty at least passably and getting it done before midnight.

The first few nights were a struggle, compounded by the fact that Josie has extremely sensitive teeth. In brushing your own teeth, of course, you can just bend over the sink and spit, but in Josie's case this was impossible. Not only was she unable to rest her hands on the sink, but there was no way for me to see inside her mouth while standing at the sink next to her. I sat her on the toilet and covered her torso with a bib, as I played at being dental hygienist. Then I used our electric toothbrush, with one hand gently brushing from tooth to tooth and the other hand holding a small plastic spittoon beneath her mouth to catch the overflow and allow her to occasionally spit. It was not a pretty picture. Often, I would have to slow down to let her catch her breath or go back to reach a tooth missed.

The real challenge came in flossing. It's difficult enough to floss my own teeth properly, holding a long strand of floss between two hands and then manipulating it in my mouth, rhythmically rubbing up and down against each tooth a half dozen times. When done correctly, it's a painfully boring task, but vital to tooth and gum health. But trying to get my two big paws and that strand of floss inside Josie's mouth proved awkward and frustrating for both of us. Fortunately, I discovered a handy little plastic tool called a dental flosser, which holds an inch or so of floss taut, so I didn't have to put both my hands in her mouth and risk choking my dear wife. Disposable plastics to the rescue, again.

Having previously experienced periodontal disease during my wasted youth, I am also a stickler for dental health and pretty much knew the drill. But the only teeth I knew were mine, and I had to fast learn about a whole new set of teeth and gums. Indeed, I can say that I know them now almost as well as my own.

Coming at the end of the day, and taking even longer than Josie's usual half hour, it was probably the most tedious task for both of us. But together we learned how to better navigate around her mouth, and gradually it became less strenuous. And when the job was finished, she would look up at me and flash a grin with her now sparkling teeth and I felt a communion with her that transcended all that had gone before. We were more than lovers and friends–we were comrades of tooth and gum forever.

After two months, the bandages came off and slowly our life returned to normalcy. Josie began to resume her daily routine, taking pride in again performing her own daily maintenance and freeing me up to go back to doing all those things I had put on hold, which in retrospect seemed less urgent. She embraced weekly sessions of physical therapy with a fierce determination to regain all her strength and ability. She had always been a strong woman, but I now watched in amazement at my new wonder woman surpassing herself each day with daily feats of recovery. And evildoers better beware of that sharp right elbow, newly reinforced with metal brace.

Our experience left us more aware of not only the possibility, but the probability, of falling as well as our ability to survive it. Not that we dwell on it. But I've noticed a certain tendency to nag, whenever one of us goes up or down the stairs without grabbing the handrail or makes too sudden a turn. According to government statistics, one out of four Americans aged sixty-five or over falls each year, and every nineteen minutes one of us will die as a result. Those are not good odds. Makes you almost afraid to go out the front door. Not what we seniors need to hear, especially when we're also told to not sit so much and to keep on moving. So, what's an old fuck to do?

For one thing, I'm going to make damned sure I don't fall. At heart I am a coward when it comes to being a care recipient. I can't begin to imagine someone having to feed, wash, and dress me each day, let alone–horrors–wipe my ass. I am sadly deficient in all the social skills my life partner possesses in spades–patience, grace, good sense, and fortitude. I know full well that, in the event I did fall, my loving spouse would be there to take care of me. All I can say is, good luck with that, Josie. I would not wish that monstrous fate on anyone.

SEX TOYS AFTER FIFTY

THE COVER HEADLINE SAID it all: "Best. Sex. Ever!" You might think it was an issue of *Cosmo*, but this was the latest *AARP The Magazine*. Though confused by the punctuation, I was hooked, especially by the subtitle: "Even in Your 70s–We Show You How."

Excitedly flipping to page 56, however, I found no steamy pictures of attractive people enjoying sex or detailed instructions on exotic sexual positions. Instead, I found a frank discussion of popular questions by AARP "sexpert" Dr. Pepper Schwartz "about how to stay frisky after 50." I did find the tip on sex toys mildly interesting, which noted that the Rabbit, the Revel Body Sonic Vibrator, and the We-Wibe "are all said to satisfy consistently."

Well, I'm no "sexpert," but I do consider myself a frisky kind of guy. After diligent, trial-and-error experimentation over the years, my equally frisky wife and I have found a few sexual toys of our own. You might want to give these a try. As far as we're concerned, forget the rabbit. For hours and hours of amusement, nothing beats a little rubber ducky in the bedroom. I'm not talking about those fancy battery-powered models–the kind that swim around in your tub and quack back at you–just a plain old yellow ducky that squeaks when you squeeze it. (This last part is particularly important. It's amazing what a little squeak can do for your orgasms.) Just imagine all the pleasures you can bring to your partner with the loving application of a little ducky. For added enjoyment, try lubricating your ducky, or have it whisper naughty little things in your partner's ear.

Still have that old Slinky toy lying around? Remember how it could magically move down a flight of stairs, end-over-end, and you'd run back up and let it go again all afternoon, never tiring of it? (OK, some of us are easily amused.) Well, forget the stairs. That same old Slinky can also perform tricks in the bedroom. Let it run down the gentle incline of your partner's spine, seductively stretching and reshaping itself. You never know quite where it'll end up.

Maybe you grew up playing with plastic dinosaurs. Well, why not bring those models into the bedroom for some Mesozoic love play? Use your little dinos as surrogate lovers to act out your most primitive fantasies. Just imagine the squeals of delight as your Tyrannosaurus gently nibbles your partner's neck.

Maybe you played with dolls instead. Maybe you still

do. Take it from us. That old Barbie and G.I. Joe can do wonders for your sex life. (Though boys usually preferred the G.I. Joe, I suspect many would have preferred the Barbie, if given a chance. How else is a boy to learn about female anatomy? Then again, you really can't learn much about a *real* female body from a Barbie.) If you tend to be shy, repressed, or lacking in imagination, dolls can be especially useful. Have Barbie and the little soldier act out new scenes and positions. Dress Barbie in a leather bra and panties and give her a whip. Have G.I. Joe, wearing his usual camouflage undies, try to fend her off, with flowers or maybe a bazooka. If you're into kinky, dress G.I. Joe in a short pink miniskirt and Barbie as Spiderman. The possibilities are endless.

While I can't guarantee these toys will satisfy everyone, they might help you loosen up a bit. They might even bring a little laughter to the bedroom, which is not a bad thing. Best of all, you don't have to visit a sex shop to buy them. You probably have a few in your closet or basement. Or steal them from your kids. They shouldn't be playing with sex toys anyway.

THE WHITEST MAN IN AMERICA

I SEE HIM EVERY DAY. He stares back at me with those blue eyes of his and pure Northern European complexion. Even his hair is now silvery, though it used to be blond. Could he *be* any whiter? For over seventy years I have put up with his boring Baltic paleness and I guess I'm stuck with him.

No, I don't wish to be black or any other color, for that matter. Still, whenever I hear the words "a person of color," I feel myself strangely incomplete and slightly envious. I see all the things I am not and never got the chance to know. What if my identity had been forged in strife rather than immunity? Imagine if my genes could express all the colors I lack. Would that my heart could feel what it's like to be ignored, beaten, raped, jailed or excluded simply because I'm not of the lighter race. If I could share, only for a moment, the bittersweet mysteries of my brothers and sisters.

As a kid, I would play cowboy with six-guns blazing at imaginary Indians, but when I watched westerns at the movies, I rooted for the Indians. The more I learned the history of our deplorable treatment of this country's original inhabitants–which continues to this day–the more ashamed I grew of my American white boy identity. But it wasn't just the outrageous immorality of it. For me, Native Americans also seemed to have the more interesting story, so different from mine. And despite being vastly outnumbered and ruthlessly hunted and corralled into reservations, they courageously fought back. For sheer bravery, cunning, and audacity, I'll take Cochise and Crazy Horse over the palefaces any day. Even famed Indian fighter George Crook grew to appreciate the noble dignity of his opponents in their doomed battle with white America.

It's the story of our country. First, take the land from the natives, and kill those who resist. Then trade some sugar and rum for slaves from Africa to do your dirty work. Breed them like cattle. Grow your economy. Then wage a fake war and steal some more real estate from the brown-skinned Mexicans. Spin your myths of the others' inferiority and brutality to justify your inhumanity. Split the country apart and spill its young men's blood till it's all over, or so you think. But it's not over, for the myths are too strong and our minds too set.

David Brooks, in an editorial for *The New York Times*, recently observed that "three-quarters of American whites have no close nonwhite friends." As for the average black person, 83 percent of his or her closest friends would be black. It would seem, he notes, that our country has entered "a phase of trepidation, or even passive segregation," and asks if there are "enough efforts to create intimate bonds across racial lines."

I do hope we get there sooner rather than later, but I am not optimistic that I'll live to see it. And how exactly do you create such bonds? Intimate bonds do not come easy.

I grew up in Manchester, Connecticut, a small city nine miles east of Hartford. During the 1950s, it was one of those racially homogeneous suburbs to which whites fled as blacks and other minorities migrated to bigger cities like Hartford in search of jobs and a better life. Census figures for 1950 show it had a population of 34,116 whites and 88 non-whites. By 1960, these figures had grown to 42,102 and 152, respectively. Hardly a demographic transition.

Even in 2000, 82.77 percent of the residents were still white, though blacks, Native Americans, Asians, Latinos and others had all made significant inroads in this mostly white "City of Village Charm."

Growing up in a city that was 99.9974 percent white, I really didn't have much of a chance as a kid to even meet a person of another race, much less establish a close friendship. I remember a couple of black teachers at the schools I attended, but that was pretty much it. It was white-bread city. I use the slang "white-bread" here not just in its racial sense but in its larger meaning as well, with all of my city's middle class striving, material values, preoccupation with outward appearances and lawn care, and sandwiches made with Wonder Bread. We were all too readily defined by the popular TV series *Leave it to Beaver.* I hated the Beaver–a whitey, goodie-two shoes twerp who was so sickeningly sweet he made me retch.

Not that there's anything wrong with middle class striving. It's OK to want to succeed, but not at the expense of other values. As a young man, I soon began to hate this suburb of my birth and all that it stood for. I found it too limited in its outlook, and far too parochial. I especially hated lawns!

I remember frequent trips with my dad to nearby Hartford, New Haven, and New York and was drawn by the fact that they were filled with people who did not look like me. Of course, I still had no clue how to make contact with them. I was given the usual advice from my parents about avoiding certain neighborhoods where more of these others lived, but as far back as I can remember, my parents never shared any racist views with us.

Thus, I was spared the parental indoctrination of racial hatred and fear that too many kids grow up with. I imagine that if I ever had managed to have a black friend or–gasp–a black girl friend, I might have heard some less than complimentary comments and perhaps even be dissuaded from pursuing the relationship. But I will never know. It just wasn't an issue we had to deal with.

After college, I briefly became a public-school teacher in my hometown, and by that time class makeup had become a little less homogeneous. I fondly remember one seventh grade black girl in my class, who got my number before I knew what was happening. She knew my sweet spot was humor and would endlessly make wisecracks at my expense. But she was so funny! Now some might call this reverse racism, for I probably never would have let any white student get away with this. But I never let it get out of hand, and neither would she. An air of discipline was maintained, while the two of us found something in the other to share, if only for a moment.

During our back to the land phase in the '70s, my wife and I purchased an old schoolhouse and 100 acres of land in the town of Landaff, New Hampshire, which at less than 400 residents arguably had more cows than people and may still have today. Not exactly a place to experience racial diversity. I thought life in Manchester was unstimulating, but this place had it beat. But then, Manchester didn't have bears, moose, and wild lonely mountains to explore.

Six years later, however, we tired of small-town life and eventually moved to Providence, Rhode Island. While not a teeming metropolis, it did at least have way more people than cows. And more people who didn't look like us.

And because it was more racially diverse than the rest of Rhode Island, it was surrounded by white flight cities and towns. I remember an incident at a predominantly white school in nearby Cranston, where courtesy of a grant from the state arts council, I had acquired a month-long writer-in-residency position. I was reading a poem from a book by Shel Silverstein, and the teacher suddenly asked me not to hold the book up, especially the back cover which displayed a photograph of the author. "I don't want them to see what he looks like," she said. I didn't say anything at the time–a fact which I regret to this day–and briefly gave her the benefit of the doubt, thinking perhaps that she simply wanted the poems to speak for themselves and for her students not to get hung up with how the poet looked.

That night, however, I went home and took a hard look at the photo on the back cover, which showed Shel's bald head and dark beard staring back in a way that *could* be construed as slightly sinister. True, he did have a dark complexion, so much so that I had to wonder. But it wasn't until years later that I Googled "Is Shel Silverstein black?" and discovered I was not alone in asking this question. Turns out, however, he was Jewish. Jesus would have had the same complexion, no doubt. But the mere fact that he didn't quite match this teacher's expectation of what a proper white person should look like really freaked her out.

My wife and I had begun to frequent the downtown blues clubs in Providence, where we got to see a number of great black musicians while mingling with a more diverse crowd. Music knows no colors or boundaries–a place where we can put aside our distrust and fear of the other for a time, if only temporarily.

Our love of blues eventually led us one night down unfamiliar dark streets to Wabash Street in downtown Chicago, to seek out *Buddy Guy's Legends*, which bills itself as "the premiere blues club in the world." We stuck our heads in the door and gazed around. It was a Monday night, but the bar was filled with patrons, most of whom appeared to be black, waiting for the show to begin. Have to confess, I felt out of place and more than a little apprehensive. What were we doing here? But then as the music started and we all began to sway in unison, the club became more like a church, filled with true believers who had come to hear the sweet soulful music.

That night happened to be an open blues jam, during which the host band plays for about an hour and then invites other local musicians on stage.

At the end of the jam, we were approached by a black musician, the late great Lefty Dizz, a Chicago blues guitarist and singer. At the time, we didn't know anything about him, other than the fact that we had enjoyed his band Shock Treatment and his wild man performance that night, laced with manic virtuoso guitar playing and raunchy jokes. Later we learned that he had released eight albums and had played with such legendary blues men as Junior Wells and Hound Dog Taylor, and had once recorded at the Checkerboard Lounge in Chicago with Muddy Waters and Mick Jagger, Keith Richards, and Ron Wood of the Rolling Stones.

He strode across the room directly toward me with a grim look on his face. Then he stopped and pointed at my Rolling Stones T-shirt. "I got some business with them Stones," he said. "They stole our songs!"

Not knowing what to do, I just shrugged and smiled nervously, suddenly questioning the wisdom of my wearing a Stones T-shirt to a Chicago blues club. Then Lefty broke into a toothy grin. "Hey, you wanna buy one of my CDs?" Which I did. We swapped jokes and jive for a time, then he continued working the room. It was one of the best nights of my life.

We eventually moved west to Arizona, in search of sunshine and new adventures. There we built a cozy cabin on five acres in the high-country foothills of Chino Valley, a small ranching and farming community just north of Prescott in Yavapai County. We had hoped it would be our retirement home, not thinking about the fact that the place we had chosen to live was one of the whitest places in Arizona and that we were again moving in the direction toward less diversity and a homogeneous neighborhood of people who looked like us.

Many of our neighbors were retirees and migrants from California, who had come to escape from a high cost of living rather than from people of color. For the most part, they were good people and not outwardly racist. But occasionally I would hear crude jokes or comments which showed that some of them liked their all-white neighborhood just the way it was.

Out of the blue one day, one of my neighbors asked me, "What's so good about diversity?" The question left me temporarily dumbfounded. Before I could launch my defense, she cut me off, expounding at length on her previous experiences and grievances with Asians in her former California neighborhood, extrapolating these to Asians everywhere. I listened and tried to present an alternative narrative, but the conversation did not go well. "I hate diversity," was her parting comment.

After a few years of this, I got so desperate to see persons with a nonwhite face that, whenever I would see them in the supermarket or post office, I had to fight the urge to go up and hug them. Not exactly the best way to make new friends. Once again, my chances of doing that were severely limited. I felt as if I were regressing into childhood, surrounded by the same kind of white folks I grew up with.

One problem with moving to the country is the tradeoff you make. Sure, it's nice to be surrounded by nature and clean air, with plenty of room to do your own thing. But that increased natural diversity comes at the cost of cultural diversity. The older I got, the more I realized how much I missed all the little interactions with others that go with living in an urban environment, all the hustle and bustle, jostling and rubbing elbows through the crowd as you go about your daily life. All the polite conversations and even the occasionally hostile ones that remind you of what being a social animal is all about. And I knew I needed these connections more than anything.

Tucked away in our little cabin in the high country, I was not making the friends I had hoped for. Sure, there were plenty of neighbors and acquaintances. But I'm talking friends here, close friends like the kind David Brooks was talking about. And the odds for me ever finding them there were not good.

I found myself increasingly thinking about friends. What does that mean, a *close* friend? Doesn't everyone have them? Give me a dozen and I'll be happy.

I guess it means having someone who's always got your back, who will listen and tell it to you like it is, who will put up with your endless shit and still be your friend. Someone with whom you can let down your guard and be vulnerable. And someone with whom you can be a complete asshole, from time to time.

On that score, I was not doing very well. I could count my close friends on one hand. I'm not counting my wife here, though perhaps I should. Married now for forty-three years, we were friends before we became lovers. And our friendship has grown deeper and closer, even when I'm sometimes an asshole.

OK, enough of this mushy stuff. What about my other close friends?

Well, there's Dan, or was, that is. Daily I mourn his passing. Another old white guy, same age as me, he was as close a friend as any man could ask for. Dan gave me my most treasured nickname–fuckhead, which always made me laugh whenever he said it. Sometimes we would sign birthday cards with FH1 and FH2, though we both knew who number one was. For a brief time, he had a promising career as a keyboardist in a Boston rock band, but confessed he had to get out of the music business for fear he would succumb to the crazy, drug-fueled lifestyle. He landed a management job in a nearby textile factory, and settled into a life of crazy semi-normalcy.

We first met at the old schoolhouse in Landaff, New Hampshire. My wife and I had just founded a local nature center offering free programs to the local community on our hundred acres. A recent membership drive had netted us some new members, including one coveted life membership for what then seemed like the princely sum of $100. As people began to arrive for one of our first weekend programs, I eyed a man with medium-length gray hair and a neatly trimmed beard get out of his car and stroll across the lawn toward the schoolhouse. I went out to greet him, and he told me his name. "So, you're our life member," I said, shaking his hand. Then as I looked into his merry eyes, there was an instant flash of recognition between us. *Why, you're as big an asshole as I am!* Now, I am not the kind who believes in love at first sight or other romantic notions. Love, like friendship, is something you have to work at. But I knew instantly, as surely as I've ever known anything, that he and I were to be lifetime buddies.

With Dan, there was a certain chemistry between us, that intimate bond that David Brooks describes. While we did share a love of rock music and the outdoors, these were incidental to what we shared, a vital honest interest in what the other was thinking or feeling, fueled at times by copious drinking and raucous humor.

Dan could bring me out of myself in ways that no one else ever has. If he knew I held something to be sacred, he would push that button relentlessly with mischievous glee. He would delight in getting me into trouble. We would go into a bar and he would strike up a conversation with a gorilla-sized guy next to us wearing a Hell's Angels jacket and then point at me and casually tell him, "He doesn't like your boots."

He was a born comedian, always pushing the

envelope of good taste. One time, we and our wives were in a crowded bar. In the middle of the room was a perfect couch for the four of us, though partially occupied at the time by two young women. Before any of us could stop him, he sat down next to them and proceeded to cough and clear his throat most disgustingly, and in no time at all the women moved. Smiling wickedly, he motioned for us to come claim our couch. For a brief moment, I felt both guilty and sad for the two women, who didn't stand a chance against Dan's protean power. I suspect they knew they had been conned out of their couch by a master and would later laugh at the episode as we did.

During his last few years, Dan worked for a local community assistance organization, helping low income county residents obtain food and fuel grants. He took great pride in his ability to help people. "They come into my office so full of anger they can barely talk," he explained to me. "But I just listen and calmly explain stuff to them, and by the time they leave it's like they're a different person." I knew exactly what he meant. Dan emitted a kind of magic alpha waves that made you a better person just by being with him.

My other close friendships were formed on the basis of shared experience rather than love at first sight. There's my friend Steve, whom I've known since kindergarten and who still lives in Connecticut. Despite a few temporary gaps when we briefly lost touch with each other, we have managed to cultivate our friendship across the miles. Like anything worth doing, it requires an investment of time and energy. But all it takes is a phone call or email, and the memories come flooding back. We grew up science nerds, with chemistry sets in the basement and slide rules on our belts, gazing at stars through small telescopes, launching homemade rockets, and setting off bombs in the neighborhood. Eventually, he made a career out of his nerdiness, becoming a chemical engineer, while I remained a science generalist.

We are different in so many ways. He's always been the precise, logical, and level-headed one, while I tend to be more emotional, wild, and unpredictable. Maybe that's what makes our friendship tick. I admired his calm rationality—a quality I've tried to cultivate over the years but sorely missing during my early years—while he envied perhaps my ability to tap and express the intense feelings that came naturally to me. He's always been the gentle Mr. Spock of *Star Trek* to my raging Dr. McCoy.

Whenever we do manage to get together, we immediately start conversing on whatever topic happens to emerge. We don't always agree, but we listen respectfully to the other and talk nonstop until one of our wives sticks her head out of the bedroom and tells us both to shut up and go to sleep.

This ability to see some quality of otherness in a person, something perhaps missing from your own life, is crucial to forming close friends. I think of my friend Jeff, whom I first met at our nature center in New Hampshire, back in the early 1980s. He worked at the time for a large state conservation group, so he and I decided to join forces in planning some joint programs for our two organizations. We both shared a passion for nature and protecting the environment, as well as for the horror stories of H.P. Lovecraft. These days, I am more of an armchair naturalist and environmentalist, while he, on the other hand, refined and cultivated his passion into a lifetime career with the National Park Service. He is currently a ranger-naturalist at Saguaro National Park in Tucson, Arizona. As things worked out, Tucson is also where my wife and I eventually settled, so now I have at least one close friend who is neither dead nor living on the other side of the country.

We get together as often as we can, enjoying lively discussions about politics, culture, and of course, nature. And sometimes we take road trips, usually to some nearby natural area. But close as I feel to Jeff, with all the shared memories, there is a gulf I cannot bridge. A true nature purist, he has read the entire *Journal of Henry David Thoreau* several times. Indeed, he lives and breathes the life of his hero. He is an intensely private man who, like Thoreau, has never married. There is a certain loneliness and ascetism about him, a firm determination to hear a different drummer and lead a more authentic life in a world which grows ever less amenable to thoughtful experiments in living. I see him on a road I will never travel and treasure that part of us we are able to share.

Now that I live in downtown Tucson–which while not exactly New York or Chicago, is more racially diverse than any place I've so far inhabited–my chances of making new friends have improved considerably. I have made many friends since we moved to Tucson, and who knows, maybe I'll eventually bond with one who's not white.

Of course, despite David Brooks' call for more "efforts to create intimate bonds across racial lines," you can't force such things. I mean, you can't exactly take out a classified ad for one, can you? "Seeking cross-racial intimate friend. (No, not *that* kind of intimate.) Someone willing to learn and grow closer from our diverse social backgrounds. Someone to listen, even when you don't agree. Someone to call when there's no one else who could possibly understand. No previous experience necessary, though you should play well with other kids and be open to developing a long-term association. Opportunities for advancement."

It would be nice if one of my new friends does turn out to be a person of color, if only for the chance to know and share a life experience most likely different from mine. So what if my friends are white or black? Why this continuing preoccupation with the myth of race?

We speak of race as if it had biological significance. Over a century ago, American sociologist W.E.B. Du Bois warned that this crude term was being used to account for differences that are more social and cultural than biological. When we start pigeonholing people into white and black groups or whatever groups, using these arbitrary classifications to justify our prejudices, we ignore the full depth and richness of human diversity. As modern genetics has borne out, again and again, race is nothing but a social construct.

Perhaps we should call it racial identity instead, how we see and define ourselves in relation to others while we hide from a truth some of us would rather deny–that we are all African, all descended from those first human ancestors who evolved on that continent millions of years ago, to eventually spread into every habitable corner of the earth. We are each a medley of gene configurations and colors, though some of us, like me, are less colorful than others.

I wish the Feds would add a category to the new census form, and instead of "Caucasian" I could just check off the box marked "all of the above."

SMALL TALK

I'M ONE OF THOSE PATHETIC, lonely guys who still does his banking in person. Sure, I could do everything online, but then I'd miss out on some great conversations.

Take this morning, for instance. I was making a simple deposit at my local bank, and was gazing off into space with what I hoped was a look of serious contemplation when the teller glanced up from his computer and asked me, "So how's *your* day going so far?"

The question startled me with its bold directness. It seemed as if the teller were trying to engage me as a real person, not just another of thousands of customers. And he wanted to know how *my* day was going?

I stared dumbfounded at the young man, who seemed as eager to hear my reply as if he were in a bar waiting for the punch line to a dirty joke. After several minutes had passed, his expression turned to concern, as beads of sweat and a look of panic appeared on my face.

You see, he didn't just ask how I am, in which case a

simple "fine, thank you" would have sufficed, but asked me how my actual day was going, which seemed to indicate that he wanted details. What really threw me, however, were those troubling last two words–"so far." This demanded some quick evaluation of how my day was progressing at this precise point in time, as measured against my general existential standard of what a good day should entail.

Franticly I considered my options. I could take the easy way out and say that it was going great *so far*, but then come back at him with that grim reminder from the Don Henley tune about how "in a New York minute everything can change." Make him think about the fragility of our daily lives and that "Nothing in the world lasts/Save eternal change." (*Honorat de Bueil, seigneur de Racan*). Maybe my teller would start worrying about what *his* day had in store for him, furtively looking behind his back and searching his car for explosives before he drove home. That would take the smile off his face.

But I think what the young man wanted was a piece of me–some little vignette in the life of the real person standing across from him. Ideally, it would involve something more interesting than the fact that I had just picked up the newspaper and had enjoyed a great walk up Fourth Avenue, except that I had stepped on some gum and been nearly stampeded by a gang of college students late for class. So I thought of some possible replies with a little more pizzazz, as for instance:

"Well, in just the past hour, I've researched my next book, visited two porn sites, made an appointment for a colonoscopy, decided which organs I wish to donate in case of my death, and was recruited by three separate terrorist organizations, one of which promised me an extra dozen virgins in heaven if I acted NOW."

Or I could take a more somber tone, tearing up and shaking my head sadly. "It was going so well between us. Just this morning, we talked about having our first child and naming him George (or Georgiana if it's a girl) after my uncle, who died from a heart attack after mistakenly taking three Viagra pills when he couldn't remember if he had taken them or not. I was so happy. Then my wife suddenly turned to me and began to sob uncontrollably. "It's all been a lie," she said. "I was going to tell you, but I didn't want to hurt your feelings." Then she told me the truth. She–I mean he–was a transvestite, which now that I think about it does explain why he had to have his own bathroom.

Or maybe I should keep it short. "How's my day going so far? Well, I've just been to my doctor and he told me that I have exactly two months to live, not counting any unused sick days or vacation time, and demanded that I pay him at the time service was rendered, meaning right now. And you want to hear the really sad part? I was stupid enough to pay him."

In the end, I decided to be honest. "Please tell your corporate masters that my day was going just great until I heard that you're raising my bank fees, and that my day would be going much better if I could get a little more interest on my CDs."

THE BIG QUESTIONS

IS THE UNIVERSE INFINITE, or do you come to a big wall with a sign that reads "End of the Road?" What is the nature of time, and can you get overtime? Is there life after death, and whatever happened to this one? What is truth, and how do I get some?

These are the questions I love to ask, which explains why I don't get invited to a lot of cocktail parties. I mean, you can't go up to someone you've just met and blurt out, "Why do we exist?" Social etiquette requires that you at least lead up to such questions with "So how do you like this weather?" or "What have you done with your face?" (OK, this last one may not be appropriate, but aren't you dying to know?)

Being a geek, I especially enjoy the big science questions. What is consciousness, for example, and how do I know that I have it? Yes, I have this brain and all those neurons and stuff, but how does that translate into an awareness that someone is staring at my breasts or unzipped fly?

Or what makes us human? We know that other animals also use tools, language, and recognize themselves in mirrors. We share 99 percent of the same genome as a chimpanzee. What makes us so special? Personally, I think it's our ability to use credit.

Is there more than one universe? Just when I think I've got a handle on how vast our universe is, some physicists propose that we might actually live in a multiverse. There could be all kinds of universes—here, there, everywhere—constantly popping into being through something called "eternal chaotic inflation," which sounds like a perpetual string of gas attacks. There could be zillions of different universes. Maybe there's one where I have an exact twin, only he's rich and famous, with six-pack abs, and can recite all the words to the song "Louie Louie." Or there's one where you *can* always get what you want.

Ever since childhood, I've been fascinated by questions about existence. I wake up and look in the mirror and see this face staring back at me, like some freak of nature. An assemblage of genes, bones, and tissues, I know that I am the unique result of a union between egg and sperm and millions of years of evolution. My thoughts identify with this thing in the mirror. Yet all of a sudden it seems odd to me that I should be here at all. What a twisted series of events it had to be that brought forth a ridiculous creature like me.

The animal books I read as a kid didn't help. I'm not talking about Peter Rabbit or Winnie-the-Pooh. I'm talking about actual animals. Certain pictures terrified me. I remember a photo of a stuffed fruit bat that scared me silly. It seemed to leer back at me from the page. The more books I read, the worse it got. Pangolins, platypuses, star-nosed moles, giraffes, okapis, giant isopods, aye ayes, blob fish, naked mole rats, narwhals, and rhinoceroses–they all seemed too bizarre to be real. How could such creatures possibly exist in the same world I inhabit? Nature must be insane.

Indeed, why should I or anything exist at all? To not exist sounds much easier. It certainly takes less energy. Some days, merely existing is all I can manage.

Some say there's a reason for existence. We're here to praise God, Allah, or Whatever. We're here because a divine force willed the universe into being. We're here because of the Big Bang. We're here out of pure luck that matter and anti-matter didn't cancel each other out at the beginning of time. We're here because the economy needs more consumers.

Of course, it could be all an illusion. How do you really know you exist? Maybe we're all just part of a story endlessly played out in some computer game. Though it may seem real to you, you may be nothing more than a made-up character. René Descartes famously declared, "I think, therefore I am." But just because you think you exist doesn't necessarily make it so.

And what's so great about existing? True, there are many advantages. Existence can be rather nice, if you can afford it. But you also have to go out and kill something to eat, get a job, reproduce, fight traffic jams, and pay taxes, unless you're a rhino, in which case someone will take your horns instead.

The worst part is, it all comes to an end. It doesn't matter whether you're a mushroom, redwood tree, sea slug, gorilla, or frazzled commuter, the result is always the same. One day you're here, the next day you're not. There is no escape clause and no returns allowed. Even stars and galaxies die in the course of their vast cosmic lifetimes.

At least your atoms will still be around. Who knows where they might end up someday–perhaps in a whale or an eagle, or some wholly new life form. Wouldn't that be something? No matter how useless your life may seem at times, it's nice to know your atoms will serve a constructive purpose in the future.

Our universe itself may die one day. I imagine it would be pretty exciting to watch, though hard to get a good seat.

For now, though, I must bid you all goodnight and go to bed. Existence is exhausting.

ALL IN THE FAMILY

"UNLOCK THE FAMILY STORY in your DNA," proclaims an ancestry website. Sounds harmless enough, so why does that fill me with dread?

Sure, I could discover there's royalty in my Lithuanian DNA, perhaps a duke or a duchess, or a brave knight who fell at the Battle of . . . wherever. More likely, however, I'll find some distant cousin who died face down on the bar floor after winning a Krupnikas-drinking contest. Perhaps a serial goat rapist or ax murderer, or some nutcase beheaded for questioning the birth certificate of King Mindaugas, the first (and only) crowned king of Lithuania.

Besides, thanks to modern science, I already know plenty about my DNA. Oh, the stories it could tell.

For one thing, I share almost 99 percent of my DNA with chimps and bonobos, and over 98 percent with gorillas. Though most of these relatives still live in Africa, I did meet one of them a few years back at the Bronx Zoo in New York. I was strolling through their Congo Gorilla

Forest exhibit, when all of a sudden there he was–a full-grown male western lowland gorilla.

He was leaning against a tree stump, gazing off into space with a forlorn expression. Stepping closer to the glass separating us–which protects them from our human respiratory diseases–I paused to look into his face. He looked back at me in a way I will never forget. For one profound moment, there was some sort of connection between us. In that great face, I saw not a gorilla, but a personable presence, someone I could relate to. I have no idea what went on in his mind. Perhaps it was: "Why aren't *you* in here instead of me?"

I've never been able to look at a gorilla in captivity since. Don't think I could handle seeing one of my relatives locked up that way, despite all the arguments for conservation and education made by zoos. Supposedly, we humans are more advanced, with our superior big brains and all. The way things are going lately, though, sometimes I feel it is our species that should be locked up.

I met another African relative–though not in the flesh–back in 2007. She, or what was left of her, was on display at the Houston Museum of Natural Science. Lucy was her name. That's what the scientists who found her fossilized bones named them, after the then popular Beatle song *Lucy in the Sky with Diamonds*. She lived over three million years ago, in what is now called Ethiopia. Though belonging to a different genus–Australopithecus–she was a fellow hominid. Next to her precious bones, the museum showed a life size model of what she might have looked like. She was much shorter than me—only three-and-a-half feet tall—with a pelvis that was all female. Her face was only a reconstructed one, but again I had that strange feeling of connectedness across the eons, that she and I were still part of the same family tree. Perhaps it was just my imagination, but she reminded me a little of my great Aunt Lavinia. Her eyes seemed to say: *We are all African.* For that is indeed where our human line branched off from other animals. Together with gorillas, bonobos, and chimpanzees, we share much of the same DNA, along with the same common ancestor.

Turns out I have oodles of relatives all over the planet. Many of them are fellow primates. Though not as close as African apes, my orangutan relations over in Borneo and Sumatra share almost 97 percent of my DNA. Not far behind are monkeys, at 93 percent. Whether I'm looking into an orangutan's face or a monkey's, it's hard not to see the resemblance, though some of them might take this as an insult.

There's even a fish, known as the zebra fish or zebra danio, with whom I share 85 percent of my DNA. A popular aquarium fish as well as research subject, this little freshwater minnow's ancestors originated on the Indian Subcontinent. Dogs, by comparison, share only 84 percent, which just goes to show that you can't always tell who your relatives are just by looking at them.

And next time you read about some new medical discovery involving some poor laboratory mice sacrificed for the good of humankind, ponder this: they share 90 percent of our DNA, which of course is why we use them in the first place, and why E.B. White's classic children's book *Stuart Little* still tugs at our heart strings.

Admittedly, some of my relatives are farther removed. For example, I share only about 60 percent of my DNA with a banana, and try as I might, I just can't see any resemblance there. With roundworms, it's only 21 percent, though I suspect some families share a much larger percentage.

Within our own species, there's only a tiny difference in DNA among all humans on earth–about 0.1 percent. Regardless of race or national origin, we are far more alike than not.

Of course, even though we may share significant percentages of our genetic material, key differences remain in how our genes are sequenced, which does explain why most members of my family gallery don't look like mice or fish (except for Uncle Vinnie). We don't even know what many of our genes do. Within the human genome, we still possess many genes inherited from our evolutionary past that are not used because they no longer serve any useful purpose. It's important not to read too much into the fact that we share some of our genes with a banana.

But the mere fact that these mutually inherited genes are there reveals a more important truth. We are *all* related—humans, apes, mice, fish, bananas, roundworms, bacteria—all life on Earth. It's right there in the fingerprints of our DNA.

According to a study published in the journal *Nature*, evolutionary geneticists have traced this material back 3.8 billion years to what is called LUCA (last universal common ancestor). This remote ancestor may have resembled the strange organisms that still exist on earth within hot volcanic vents found deep under the oceans. Talk about long distant relatives. But from that ancient trunk would eventually spread the branches of our tree of life. It's all in the family.

HOW TO CHOOSE THE PERFECT GOD

IT'S NOT LIKE GOING INTO a store and selecting a new sofa or mattress, though come to think of it, you should look for something comfortable and durable. Most of us never get a chance to choose a god we can live with. We grow up with the religion we're assigned at childhood, and by the time we reach adulthood it's too late. Some of us ignore or eventually grow out of it. Others suffer a wrenching existential crisis when they discover that the religion that once sustained them no longer provides answers. And some decide to just go with the flow and settle into a comforting complacency of lukewarm faith.

Too bad we're not provided at childhood with intensive training on all the many options available in choosing a religion or god. Instead of being brainwashed in the religion of their parents, kids would take comprehensive comparative religion courses, beginning with basic preschool stuff about the actual meaning of the word "god" and what that entails. As they advance, they would learn what to look for in a god, and how to recognize a good deal when they see it.

To start with, just what is a god supposed to be? An all-powerful being, some would say. But that's hardly a sufficient answer, even for a three-year-old. How powerful? Can it do tricks? Can it make things, like the Earth and stars and planets? At the very least, you want a god that can create *everything*. You don't want some lesser god like a nymph. Nymphs are gentle Greek deities in charge of protecting springs, forests, meadows, trees and other local features, but I doubt they could create a mouse, much less a dinosaur.

Durability is important. You want a god that goes the distance, and won't crap out on you after five years, or 100,000 miles, whichever comes first. Some gods do offer a lifetime warranty, though the price can be steep.

A factor not often discussed is portability. Say you decide to change your religion. Can you take your chosen god with you to your new religion? There's talk now of making insurance policies portable from job to job. You would think there would be portable gods as well. Sad to say, this is not the case. You're pretty much stuck with the religion's own brand of god. Suppose you really dig the Egyptian god Hathor, otherwise known as the Cow Goddess, who is sometimes depicted as having a woman's body and a cow's head. You can't just take her with you if you suddenly convert to Islam or

Christianity. Each of these religions will invariably insist that you immediately drop Hathor and worship *their* god. It's a pity, since allowing followers to bring along as many gods as they please would certainly help to liven up religions and make worship more fun.

And how tough is this god? Can it beat the crap out of other gods in a fight? You don't want a wimpy god.

Take the Hebrew god Yahweh of the *Old Testament*. He doesn't like what people are doing, so he makes a big flood and wipes out every creature on earth except for those onboard an ark. Now *there's* a tough god!

But I wonder just how tough Yahweh would be if he had to go a round or two with the Hindu god Shiva the Destroyer. Supposedly, he goes around destroying not only all life but the whole universe just so it can be re-created. He is said to have a third eye, the source of all his wild energy. He wears a cobra necklace and animal skins, and wields a mean-looking trident. Yahweh, on the other hand, appears as a burning bush.

This brings up another problem. Once you have chosen and accepted a god, you can't help trying to visualize this god. That might work for Greek gods, who are viewed as merely glorified versions of humans. But if yours is a Christian god, it is generally believed to be transcendent (outside space and time), totally incomprehensible, and incorporeal (all spirit with no body). So just how the hell are you supposed to visualize it?

Raised as a Catholic, I had to take the god I was given, the one true Catholic one, or so my catechism said. I was told that god (in fairness to other gods, I am not using capitals) was infinite, mysterious, and beyond anything I could possibly imagine. That didn't stop me from trying. When I prayed and stared at the altar in church, I tried to imagine this pure, milky-white, all-encompassing emptiness at the center of all being. In other words, a big fat nothing. I needed more.

Fortunately, there were plenty of visual aids. Catholics are big on icons, which can include crosses, statues, carvings, pictures, and even little plastic figurines you mount on the dashboard to keep you safe. Some Muslims don't like this, claiming that crucifixes or statues of saints constitute idolatry, the worship of these items as if they were the real thing. But just as in Buddhism, Hinduism, and Jainism, Catholics use these objects merely to better focus the mind on what they're supposed to be worshipping, sort of a heaven's little helper. The problem is, you end up limited by this all too imperfect depiction of the divine.

As a kid, I would look at a statue or picture of Jesus and imagine that he was actually a long-haired, bearded, white hippie in sandals, like some cool guy at Woodstock. But he always seemed kind of wimpy to me. I couldn't imagine him chasing the money changers out of the temple. And he had always had a sorrowful face. Didn't he ever laugh? Paintings of god the father showed an old, gray-haired and fleshier version of a white guy, as if Jesus had just grown up. Who decided that God is white? And always a man, not a woman? As for the Holy Ghost, what's with that? Sounds like Halloween. At least put a sheet on him and *show* him as a ghost, not some silly white dove.

And while I was stuck with these limited male images of god, other religions had all kinds of cool deities. I especially loved Hinduism, where you have Ganesha, with an elephant's head and round human body. And they have female gods, too! There's that divine female known as Devi, and fair-skinned Sarasvati, all dressed in white. Better yet, there's full-bosomed Lakshmi, the goddess of wealth, with her broad hips and warm smile. I can just hear her saying, "Why don't you come up some time, and see me?" Gods don't have to be limited in their attributes.

You also want a god who doesn't require too much of you. It's all right for a god to expect a little acknowledgement and maybe an occasional thanks now and again, when things are going well. But I would definitely draw the line at those Mayan gods who require regular human sacrifice. Now some people might find this has a certain cachet. Not me. If I have to kill someone to worship you, well, that's unacceptable. Even a god who says such a thing, but doesn't really mean it, is not to be trusted. Whenever I heard that story in the *Old Testament* about god telling Abraham to kill his only son, I thought, "What kind of god would even suggest such a thing?" It totally creeped me out. Supposedly this was symbolic foreshadowing of the promised son of god to come, who would be sacrificed for the good of humanity, but for me the damage was done. Then god tells Abraham to just go kill a poor ram instead, and everything's fine. Well, it ain't. Killing animals shouldn't be a requisite, either. As for the son of god metaphor, you'd think an infinitely powerful god would find a better way to communicate with his subjects than staging such a sophomoric act. Downright sloppy.

So, what kind of requirements should you look for? At one end of the spectrum, you have gods who are content with a little chanting and dancing, general detachment, and just going with the flow, with maybe a little meditation thrown in. You can easily fit that in after work and still have the whole weekend free for less divine pursuits.

Watch out, though, for the Mormon god, who demands that you abstain from alcohol, tobacco, coffee, and tea, and must marry for eternity (marrying for life is hard enough). The Rastafarian god may insist you wear dreadlocks. The Nation of Islam god requires you to pray five times a day. He also requires that you respect all laws, don't make war, and not bear arms, the last which some Second Amendment folks might find hard to obey. The Gnostic god requires strict celibacy and asceticism, since all matter is considered evil. This might explain the fact that this religion is pretty much extinct.

For minimal obligation, nothing beats the Deist god who, being totally uninterested in the world, doesn't require you to do a goddamn thing. He doesn't want to hear about your whiny needs, either, so don't bother praying to him.

One final thing to look for. You definitely want a god who is cool. Now I'm going to say something here which could get me stoned or shot, so you'd better step back. I always had trouble thinking of Jesus as cool. Yeah, he was supposed to have performed all those miracles, like turning water into wine—a neat trick, I must admit. But his mother had to beg him to do it, to which he replied, "Woman, what does this have to do with me? My hour has not yet come." Jesus Christ! You're talking to your mother, dude. He was a real boor at parties, always telling people how they're going to hell for this or that, with never a nice thing to say about anyone. He did save that woman condemned of adultery who was about to be stoned. Having broken up the mob, he told her that he won't condemn her, either. Then he ruined it by telling her to sin no more. So judgmental. OK, so he had a lot on his plate. But I think he could have found time occasionally to joke around, maybe go out drinking with his disciples, show some cool dance moves at a wedding, and simply be human. I just couldn't relate to him.

Here are a couple of imaging suggestions for a cool god. Imagine her as Lady God, in the form of Billie Holiday, at the top of her fame, singing her divine, jazzy songs "God Bless the Child" and "Strange Fruit." All she would require of us is that we sing to one another. A case could also be made for Frank Sinatra or Queen front man Freddie Mercury, either of whom would be a lot more fun and inspirational than some wimpy, goody-goody hippie in robe and sandals or that fat old guy on the ceiling of the Sistine Chapel.

Personally, I can't think of a better image than that of Louis Armstrong, or Lord Satchmo, as his followers call him. Just imagine him creating the world with a blow of his sweet trumpet, then singing softly to himself, "What a Wonderful World."

TO PROCREATE OR NOT

A FEMALE WHITE RHINO, on average, can produce eleven offspring during her lifetime. Who knows how many more are sired by the male rhino . . . or Mick Jagger, for that matter? A nine-banded armadillo can produce fifty-four, while lemmings and rabbits can produce hundreds. Spreading your genes around is the first rule of life. From an evolutionary standpoint, I'm a complete failure.

The closest I ever got to procreating was in my early twenties when the young woman I was dating and hoped to marry asked me pointblank if I wanted to have children. Yes, I told her, of course. I even convinced myself that I really did. Men will do anything to get a woman into bed.

Fortunately for both of us, she saw through me (the fact that at the time I was employed in a pet shop, dreaming about all the successful books I would write, may have also made her think twice about my future financial prospects). We went our separate ways, sparing me not only thousands of dollars on an engagement ring worthy of my potential fiancé's expensive tastes, but the inconceivable tragedy of my becoming a parent.

Growing up, I never thought much about having kids. I just didn't see it as a life goal, the way some people have always known that they wanted to be parents. *I want exactly seven–three boys and three girls and one . . . well, whatever the Good Lord gives us–dealer's choice.*

Occasionally I caught myself thinking about what it might be like. Taking my little boy or girl hiking. Trying to explain the mysteries of sex or how to fry an egg. Passing on my genes and values to some little person with maybe the same blue eyes and big ears, who would for a time worship the ground I walk on and demand all my waking moments, then completely ignore me in her teens, and later call me a terrible drunken monster when she wrote her memoir at thirty-two.

According to a 2013 Gallup poll, over half of all U.S. citizens eighteen to forty already have kids, and even the 40 percent who don't still hope to have them someday. Only six percent of this group do not want to have any children, under any circumstances. Seems I'm in the minority.

But at least among the seventy-five million or so millennials in this country, I have company. According to a recent Cassandra report, fully a third of them do not want kids. Many see this as a deliberate lifestyle choice or not wanting to take on the significant responsibilities that go with parenting. And they don't seem at all worried about what people will think. Gotta love those millennials.

Of course, if your spouse or significant other really wants kids, it's hard to say no. I could very well have ended up reproducing, whether I wanted to or not, had I not had the incredible good fortune of meeting and marrying my one and only wife, Josie. She never wanted kids, either. How lucky was that!

I realize that, if every human on the planet shared my views, we would soon go extinct, which might not be a bad idea, considering how our species has totally messed up the planet. We're not exactly the pinnacle of evolution. We've had long enough to change our ways. Why not put some other species, preferably with more intelligence, say ravens, elephants, or even white rhinos, in control of things? The earth would do just fine without us, as it has for billions of years.

Could be I'm just lacking a baby gene. While other people gush about how cute the new baby is, I'm heading for the door, especially if pictures are involved. The only thing worse than kiddie pictures are dog pictures. Let me know how the kid (or dog) turns out at twenty-one, *then* we'll talk. And face it, some babies are about as cute as a newborn naked mole rat.

I could blame my attitude on my maternal grandmother, whom I adored, having spent many idyllic early days on her farm. I remember her warning me how the world was getting worse every day and never to bring kids into this world. Of course, she could have been just tired of putting up with all her own kids' crap–she had four–or with me, for that matter. I was always getting into trouble, shooting fish and frogs in her pond with my BB gun or cutting down trees in the woods with my ax and leaving three-foot-tall stumps (well, she did ask me to clear out some of the shrubs and trees encroaching on the field).

Not that it's likely, but I can think of several good reasons why I shouldn't procreate. First of all, my wife still doesn't want to. And I doubt very much if she would approve of me spreading my seed around, even if it might potentially benefit the human gene pool. It also sounds like a lot of work, and would impinge on my afternoon naptime.

Second, if I ever did have a kid–perish the thought–I would undoubtedly be a terrible father, the kind who thinks the only good music is classic rock and embarrasses his kids by continuing to wear in public tight Rolling Stones T-shirts over his advancing pot belly.

Finally, there are plenty of people who still want to have kids, as well as plenty who have them accidentally. There are far too many of us here already, with more on the way. Way I see it, I'm doing my bit for the planet. The two, four, six (hey, why not twelve, as long as we're being hypothetical?) kids Josie and I *might* have had are a counterbalance to those being born. Plus, I've kept my genes out of the gene pool, which on further reflection is probably a good thing. One Gene is quite enough.

SHOUTING MY ABORTION

I'VE ALWAYS BEEN A T-shirt kind of guy, wearing my shirts to proclaim allegiance to everything from favorite rock groups to science, humor, politics, and the organizations I support, including Planned Parenthood. My collection currently includes four PP shirts, and I wear them proudly whenever I can. While some might view this as confrontational, I see it as a potential means to open up communication. Most of the time, people don't even notice. Occasionally, though, someone will notice, as for instance when someone thanks me for wearing my shirt. So far, no one has vocally challenged me, but every once in a while, I get one of those icy stares—the kind that bore straight through you. Even a stare has value, however, in that someone who may not support Planned Parenthood must still acknowledge the fact that here is someone who does—a male, no less. Besides, my wife thinks I look good in pink. How can I argue with that?

When I first saw a photo of my hero Gloria Steinem

wearing an "I had an abortion" T-shirt, my first thought was, I want one, too. The shirt was designed by Jennifer Baumgardner, co-producer of the award-winning 2005 documentary *I Had an Abortion.* The photo was taken by Tara Todras-Whitehill, who contacted Baumgardner and suggested photographing all of the women in the film wearing their "I had an abortion" T-shirts.

I did find a men's version of the shirt still available online, though the merchant warned me that it was "controversial," a fact which has never stopped me before.

There is one slight problem, however. As far as I can remember—and I'm sure I would if I did—I've never actually had an abortion. It would require that I first get pregnant. Since I'm a male human—not a seahorse or a pipefish—there's little chance of that occurring.

I sometimes wonder what would happen if men could get pregnant. We may find out soon. The Cleveland Clinic has just performed the first successful uterus transplant in the U.S. The operation involves transplanting a temporary uterus, allowing women who either were born without a uterus or have suffered irreversible uterine damage to eventually become pregnant and give birth. In the not too distant future, it may even be technically feasible to implant a uterus in a man as well, so that he could become pregnant.

If and when such a procedure does become reality, there will undoubtedly come a time when a pregnant man decides, for one reason or another, to terminate his pregnancy. Would our opinion toward abortion then change? It might not become a "sacrament," as Gloria Steinem and Florynce Kennedy famously suggested. But I suspect abortion would take on a whole new meaning.

Being a guy, I can just imagine what some future male might say. "No way you're going to tell me what to do with my body. I'm king of my castle." When some legislator tried taking his abortion rights away, he would stand his ground and shout: "You and whose army?" When accused of getting pregnant because of rape, carelessness, or lascivious attire, he would undoubtedly scream his innocence like John Belushi to Carrie Fisher in the 1980 movie *The Blues Brothers*: "It's not my fault!"

Women of today voice similar thoughts–if in different terms–though their words are often ignored. We may have come a long way toward achieving full equal rights, but we're still a male-dominant culture in far too many ways.

As part of that culture, I'll never have to worry about someone trying to control my womb or dissing me for having an abortion. But what if I could get pregnant? How would I feel?

For starters, I would want abortion to be fully accessible as an option–for me, my friends, my family, *anyone*, with no questions or restrictions. I would want it available 24-7 as a potentially life-saving procedure because, well, *I might die*, since "the risk of death associated with childbirth is approximately fourteen times higher than that with abortion." I would not want my body ever considered a mere vessel for childbirth, with fewer rights than the fetus within me. I would not look down on those who decide to have an abortion—for whatever the reason—or think that their moral view of abortion is inferior to mine. And I would not let some religion or government dictate what I should believe about abortion. (Indeed, if I ever did have an abortion, I would want to shout it from the rooftops because it was my decision and the right thing for me to do.)

I refuse to believe abortion is "an absolute evil," as Pope Francis recently described it. Nor do I think of it as a necessary evil, as even some abortion rights defenders sometimes refer to it. Evil is one of those loaded words I try to avoid. The Oxford Dictionary defines evil as "morally bad and cruel" or "having a harmful effect on people." Abortion is neither bad nor cruel. While it does involve terminating a growing, still developing fetus that might one day become a baby, that doesn't change the fact that it is sometimes necessary or prudent. And it can have an enormously beneficial effect on the person having an abortion.

According to a frequently cited 2011 study by the Guttmacher Institute, 30 percent of women (almost one in three) will have an abortion by age forty-five. Admittedly, this study was based on 2008 abortion rates. Since abortion rates have declined since 2008—perhaps as a result of better access to health care and more efficient birth control methods–it is quite possible that this percentage will be somewhat lower in the future. Whether the rate of abortion ultimately goes up or down, for now the data "suggests it is not an uncommon procedure. It is likely that a substantial proportion of patients seen by many obstetricians and gynecologists will have had an abortion or will have one in the future." In other words, it's a significant portion of the population. Odds are abortion is closer and more personal than you realize. How can we stigmatize something that affects the lives of so many of us?

An online merchant offers a T-shirt with a variation on this message, proclaiming "Someone You Love Had an Abortion."

I think I found my new T-shirt.

THE UNILLUSTRATED MAN

CALL ME A FREAK. Not a hippie freak, eco-freak, or Jesus freak, just a plain old freak. You see, I don't have a tattoo. Yesterday I saw a geezer (i.e., someone older than I) downtown–he had to be at least 97–with a big red heart on his neck and the word "Alice," which I thought was kind of sweet until I noticed just above it a raised hand holding a dagger. Some guys never get over their divorces.

A recent Harris poll found that 21 percent of U.S. adults now have a tattoo, and among the younger crowd it's almost twice that. It won't be long before Pope Francis has one–I suspect he secretly does–and there'll be no unadorned skin left on the planet. Freaks like me will be eyed suspiciously. *Why doesn't that man have a tattoo? Is he trying to make a statement? It's un-American, I tell you!*

It's not that I don't think tattoos are cool. I am fascinated by the diverse and creative ways we set ourselves apart from the herd. When I see some young dude with green-streaked purple hair wearing barbed wire around his neck, twenty pounds of nose, ear, lip, and throat jewelry, and his skin adorned with the full complement of body art, I get all warm and fuzzy inside. How difficult it must be these days to achieve that perfect rebellious, insolent, don't-give-a-damn look. It's all about making a statement.

When I was a kid, the only tattoos I remember were those on the arms of my two ex-navy uncles. The rule was, if you were in the navy, jail, a carnival, or a gang you got one. But then, during the '60s, tattoos really took off in this country as part of a cultural reaction to the values of the white, straight, middle class. Pretty soon, tattoos weren't just for stoned-out rock musicians or starving artists. Middleclass and upper-class folks started sporting them. The rest is history. The prevailing culture simply swallowed up the protest symbol. Tattoos are now just something to do. When you see a tattooed politician, stock broker or brain surgeon riding to work on his Harley, you know the tattoo has lost any shock impact it once possessed.

It won't be long before the tattoo gestapos find me. They'll haul me into some back-alley tattoo parlor and force me to undergo body art, and probably some piercing, too.

I've decided to be proactive. Rather than allowing them to put some tacky tattoo of Mickey Mouse, Miley Cyrus, or worse on my arm, I'll have a design all worked out. That way, when they come crashing through the front door, I'll have something to show them. They might go easier on me, knowing that I've put a little thought into it.

Being a poet, I thought I could have one of my little poems inserted under my skin in tasteful script, on a part of my body normally exposed. I don't mind sharing my poems, but having to take my shirt off to let someone read a poem is too great a price to ask of my art. Of course, there's always the risk of would-be poetry critics coming up to me and provoking a scene. *It doesn't rhyme. How it can it be poetry? He obviously took that line straight out of Frost.*

Perhaps I could reproduce some famous paintings for my body art. I can see one arm sporting Monet's *Les Quatre Arbres (Poplars),* while the other features Botticelli's *The Birth of Venus.*" On my neck (my legs are too hairy) I could have Goya's *Saturn Devouring His Son.* That would get some attention. I do worry, however, that the aging canvas upon which they are painted would sag and fade with time, requiring extensive restoration.

I need a bold statement, something that will really stand out. Since I live in Arizona, why not get a brand burned into my flesh. It needs to be simple and concise, something that reveals who I am–maybe a little heart with the words "Irreverent Infidel" or "In Silliness We Trust." For once in my life, I might actually get ahead of the curve. These days, it's all about branding.

AGING AWKWARDLY

IN A FEW DAYS, I'll be sixty-eight—a little closer to staring off into space while drooling uncontrollably (actually, I'm already doing that), a little closer to that final scattering of my molecules into places unknown, which does sound kind of fun.

According to data compiled in 2011 by the Organization for Economic Co-operation and Development (OECD), U.S. citizens have an average life expectancy of 78.7 years. I could move to Slovenia, where it's 80.1 years, but I doubt it'd be worth it.

So, with any luck, I should be around for at least another 10.7 years as long as I don't do something stupid, like wingsuit flying or free soloing. I've also got good genes, since both my parents lived into their nineties. So stick it, OECD!

I'm still left with the fact, however, that I've used up a good two-thirds of my life or more. Not sure if Einstein would have agreed, but time does move faster relative to the amount you have left, the closer you get to that big black hole that awaits all of us.

Forget that Robert Browning claptrap: "Grow old along with me! / The best is yet to be." While all signs indicate that I am certainly not growing younger, damned if I'll sit back and wait for decrepitude to overtake me. Acquiescence is just not my thing. As for the supposedly greater wisdom that comes with age, I'd much prefer the libido and strength of my twenties.

We are bombarded with advice on how to accept our limitations and age gracefully. A recent CNN article (*The secrets to aging gracefully*) says I shouldn't hide behind makeup (which I don't, though on some guys it looks great) and that I should ditch the spa (never tried one, unless having egg on my face counts as a facial). People who age gracefully, it says, "exude confidence." All I can manage is a little false hope before breakfast. They are also "up on the latest trends," which means my Led Zeppelin T-shirts are out. As far as not being afraid to embrace my grays, how about silver?

Another article says that to live longer I should get plenty of sleep (check), avoid too much stress (check), and that I should not consume more than two alcoholic drinks per day (OK, forget that one). And, oh yes, aim to have sex at least once a week (actually I added that one, which does sound like a good idea).

When it comes to aging, I think the pundits have it all

wrong. "Gracefully" sounds too accepting, like Fred Astaire or Ginger Rogers dancing off into the sunset. No one's ever compared me to Fred (Ginger maybe, but not Fred). I'll just muddle along like always, making up the dance as I go along, tripping over my feet as I forget where I'm going. One thing I do know. I'm going to age as awkwardly as I've lived, lurching this way or that, higgledy-piggledy.

So, I've come up with a few tips of my own. Make some noise every once in a while, just to let people know you're not dead yet. For me, it's cranking up some AC/DC or Stones (no soft rock allowed!). Let the neighbors know you're there, though preferably not after nine p.m.

Do something silly–not stupid–every day. Silliness requires that you step outside of yourself and do something that makes no sense at all. Do it because it makes you laugh. Do it because it makes those around you think you're nuts, which is part of the idea. It's a kind of creative defiance that turns the world around a little, if only for a moment. And it doesn't cost anything, unless you get fined for drawing a silly face on your tax return.

Part of being human is making an occasional ass of yourself, but try not to make a career out of it. I don't care how respectable and careful you are. At some point in your life, you're going to be an ass. I'm sure Pope Francis is a cool, upstanding guy, but even he must look back on some of his early days and say, "Boy, what an ass I was!" And look at St. Augustine. He got to have all that fun being an ass, then confessed it all and became famous. It's OK to be an ass once in a while, but eventually you have to own up to it and take responsibility.

And since everyone is an ass sometimes, try not to be too critical. Your turn will come soon.

Some final tips. If you do a lot of drinking, it's best that you not keep guns around the house. And if you can no longer laugh at yourself or face another day, do like an old dog and go off quietly to die in the woods. Don't blow your brains out in the kitchen. Have some sympathy for the cleaning crew.

MY INTERVIEW WITH TERRY GROSS

I CAN SAY WITH CONSIDERABLE certainty that I will never be interviewed by Terry Gross on *Fresh Air*, unless perhaps I publish a string of blockbuster slasher/romance novels or become the first human male to give birth to a gorilla. Still, a man can dream. Here's how it might go.

Terry: Today I'm interviewing author Gene Twaronite, as part of our new series on writers you've never heard of. Hi, is this Gene? I'll be doing the interview with you today.

Me: Yes, this is Gene. Wow, I can't believe it's really you! I'm so excited to be on your program. I'm a huge fan. I can't tell you how many times I've fantasized about–

Terry: Yes, yes, let's get on with it, shall we? Gene, could you tell us how you feel about the fact that you are currently ranked the nine millionth most popular author on Amazon, just behind Arthur Slobnick, who wrote a book of Christmas verse for his dog?

Me: Writing isn't all about fame and money, Terry–

is it OK if I call you that? It's about expressing yourself, and sharing your words with others. It doesn't matter how many books you sell or who's heard of you. The important thing is that you've created something unique in the world. To quote a poem by Shel Silverstein: "Put something silly in the world that ain't been there before." And by the way, my rank this morning is actually 8,997,332, but who's counting?

Terry: I've always loved that poem and yes, your stuff is pretty silly. So, you don't care that no one has heard of you and you make only a two-figure income? And please call me Ms. Gross.

Me: Sorry, Terry, I mean Ms. Gross. Well, sure, I wouldn't mind selling a lot more books or receiving some literary acclaim. But it's really about living an authentic life and putting your work out there. Long after I'm gone, my books will live on, bringing enjoyment to new generations of readers.

Terry: Gene, now don't take this the wrong way, but it's unlikely your books will live on if no one buys and reads them. They'll just fade away in the cloud. You'll be one more of the tens of millions of writers who aspired to fame and lost. Fifty years from now, no one will have heard of you. There will be no trace of your ever being here.

Me: Gee, Ms. Gross, you really know how to hurt a guy. Yet you say it in such an upbeat, caring voice.

Terry: Sorry, Gene–reality sucks. You and all the

other authors out there need to hear the truth. You're never going to be number one on Amazon. Stop living in a dream world. Maybe there are other things you could do.

Me: Excuse me, Ms. Gross, but when are you going to ask me about my books?

Terry: OK, we still have oodles of time to fill and as long as I've got you here, let me ask you about your first novel *The Family That Wasn't.* Your main character, John Boggle, has this crazy hyphenated name: Bazukas-O'Reilly-Geronimo-Giovanni-Li Choy-Echeverria. Weren't you worried about offending people with hyphenated names? It sounds like you're making fun of them. Do you ever get complaints from them?

Me: Actually, I was trying to show why this family I had invented was so crazy that they insisted on keeping all those names. I wasn't trying to make fun of anyone but these fictional characters. No one's ever complained, but thanks to your question they probably will now.

Terry: Your sequel *My Vacation in Hell* must have been really tough to write. You show John Boggle being sexually abused by his fake Uncle Vinnie. The experiences you describe are so vivid. Tell me, were you ever sexually abused?

Me: You know, that's the first thing my wife asked when she first read it. It's as if she thought I couldn't write such realistic scenes without actually having had the experience, and she's my biggest fan. But no, to the best of my knowledge, I was never abused.

Terry: Still, you must have felt something as you wrote those disturbing sex scenes. I know that, as a writer, you have to project yourself into the life of your characters, to feel what they feel. Now you don't have to answer this if it makes you uncomfortable in any way, but were you sexually aroused while writing them?

Me: OK, in the first place, it is perfectly possible to write about sex without getting physical. Second, I do find your question offensive. Is that something you ask all your guests? Did you ask Hillary or Bill O'Reilly about *their* sexual life?

Terry: Well, it does sometimes help to keep the conversation going. Sorry if I offended you, and no, I didn't ask them that, but maybe I should have. Can just see the look on old Bill's face. Well, I see our time is about up. Our guest was author Gene Twaronite. I really enjoyed talking to you, Gene. Could you tell us a little about your next book? Oops, sorry—out of time. Best of luck to you. Bye.

LIVING THE ABSURD LIFE

A FRAMED QUOTE BY Albert Camus hangs over my desk: "The absurd is the essential concept and the first truth." To which I would add, but can it dance?

It is not a question Camus might have asked. In fact, it's ridiculous. It just popped into my head, like so many other wacky thoughts. Cultivating such silliness is a strategy I've found most helpful during times of darkness and despair.

This intentional silliness is what many of us think of when we hear the word "absurd." Unfortunately, many people also have a negative view of the absurd, since it involves a deliberate violation of what we consider reasonable, leading to illogical, nonsensical, often bizarre situations. Totally unpredictable, it follows no rules, turning on its head everything we hold logical and true. And some of us don't like that.

Absurdist, or surreal, humor is the heart of all great comedy. Think of the preposterous scene from Lewis

Carroll's *Alice's Adventures in Wonderland,* in which Alice attempts to play croquet using a flamingo as mallet and a hedgehog for a ball. Or Edward Lear's "Owl and the Pussy-Cat" sailing off to get married and eating slices of quince with a runcible spoon? What exactly is a runcible spoon? Or Franz Kafka's novella *Metamorphosis*? You can't get more ridiculous than waking up and suddenly finding yourself having turned into a giant cockroach. Then there's Samuel Beckett's absurdist play *Waiting for Godot,* in which two characters, Vladimir and Estragon, wait for a guy named Godot who never shows up and nothing really happens. But oh, what a glorious nothing it is! More recently, comics George Carlin, Jonathan Winters, Robin Williams, and Monty Python, to name a few, have shared their private worlds of wackiness and helped to keep us sane.

But this silliness quite often masks a deep sadness, alienation, and inner struggle. Lewis Carroll used absurd humor as a way to deal with the chaotic changes taking place during the Victorian period when, much like in Alice in Wonderland, the traditional British life he had known was being turned upside down. So he showed his character Alice struggling to make sense of this ever more curious world that she must navigate.

Camus meant something entirely different by the absurd, which can also mean "the quality or condition of existing in a meaningless and irrational world." According to him: "There is only one really serious philosophical question, and that is suicide." Silly was not his game. Talk about depressing. Can you imagine this guy at a dinner party? Instead of the usual banter, he would stare, with eyes ablaze, at the guests around the table and ask, "What is the meaning of existence?" And as each cited their various religious, philosophical, scientific, and personal answers, Camus would knock them down, one by one.

Ever the skeptic, he would insist that there is no adequate answer to this question. Despite all our efforts to find purpose to our existence, the universe remains silent on this issue. We cannot reason our way to meaning, he argued, for "this world in itself is not reasonable." Considering the vast, ever-expanding amount of information available to us as well as all that may forever remain unknown makes total certainty beyond our grasp.

Camus rejected the false hope and comfort offered by religion. Like the philosopher Nietzsche, he saw the danger of devaluing this life at the expense of an afterlife which may never come. Why deprive ourselves of the rich opportunities offered by a life we know for one which we cannot know for certain? And therein lies the dilemma. While our human hearts seek to find purpose and meaning to it all (as in Dionne Warwick's song "What's It All About, Alfie?"), there is no definitive answer, no "familiar, calm surface which would give us peace of heart" This is what Camus means by the absurd.

In his classic work *The Myth of Sisyphus*, Camus provides us with the memorable image of a man doomed for eternity to push a boulder up a hill only to have it roll back each time it reaches the top. Sisyphus is the absurd human, doomed to struggle through life without hope or meaning.

According to Camus, you have two choices. Deal with this emptiness in your soul and embrace it, with no hope of escape or consolation, while boldly seeking your own meaning, or decide you can't deal with it and just end it.

Camus saw death as "the most obvious absurdity," so he chose life instead. Through his writing, and his personal and political life, he defiantly resisted the apparent meaninglessness of existence. During World War II, he joined the French Resistance to help liberate Paris from Nazi occupation, and edited the underground newspaper *Combat*. In 1957, he was awarded the Nobel Prize for Literature. Though his life was cut tragically short, he showed us a way to triumph over despair and live an authentic life with dignity.

I must admit, I do sometimes feel like Sisyphus, pushing my personal rock up the hill only to see it come crashing down again, experiencing times when everything I do seems hopeless and my life seems to have as much purpose as the floppy disk I found wedged between a copy of *The Hobbit* and *The Oxford Book of Modern*

Verse. Unlike Camus, however, the question that comes to mind is not: should I kill myself?

I do agree with Camus that the world is not reasonable, and find it curious that I am here. I look in the mirror and see a creature no less bizarre than a giraffe or a star-nosed mole, with all those weird tentacles at the end of its nose. As a kid, I used to gaze at pictures of certain animals in books and shudder. How could they be? They seemed so unreal.

And here am I, as improbable as Ionesco's rhinoceros running through the streets. My face stares back at me in disbelief. I feel a disconnect between the image in the mirror and the image I carry inside. Is it really the same me, with all those dreams, lusts, and ambitions, all those noble and idle thoughts, all those precious and hateful memories? Or is it a mirage of someone who once was? As I write this, countless cells in my body have died and been replaced, as neurons flash and chart new pathways and memories in my brain. The person I saw this morning is no more.

Tomorrow I will look in the mirror again, and what will I see? Will I see "the master of my fate" and "the captain of my soul?" Or will I see the more usual face of befuddlement and despair?

It is the dance I perform each day–a dance for meaning–and I never know how it will turn out. Some days, it's a little jig before breakfast. Other days, it's more like a polka from hell, or a slow, sad waltz on my grave.

Most often, it begins with some little thing. A little ray of hope that sets my feet moving. Some encouraging thought or word from a friend. An inspiring poem or essay. Some newly discovered truth I had forgotten. A piece of news that proves the world is not coming to an end . . . not yet, at least.

And I remember that the purpose of my life does not come from external sources. There is no guidebook or grand plan, no voices telling me what to do. Rather it is a series of little daily steps I take to keep the darkness at bay. It's realizing the value of simple things, like kindness, empathy, and understanding. Expanding my mind with new insights and knowledge. Exulting in the awe of this wondrous universe and the fact that, for a little while, I am here to experience it. Writing the best I can, relishing the little triumphs while accepting that I will never be as good as Shakespeare, Yeats, or Steinbeck. James Baldwin famously wrote: "I want to be an honest man and a good writer." That's as good a credo to live by as any.

But there are times when I lose sight of these and all seems lost, and the only thing that can save me is silliness. Not some tired slapstick silliness, but the kind that's absurd to the bone and makes you laugh so hard you start blowing things out your nose.

Humor is highly subjective, of course, but there's a scene in the movie *Monty Python and the Holy Grail* that gets me every time. The knights appear to be riding around on invisible horses as their squires clap coconuts together to produce the sound of hoof clopping (it was a low budget movie and the group didn't have enough money to afford actual horses, or so they say). And you want to know what's really absurd? Watching the movie, I begin seeing the horses. When and if nuclear war breaks out, I will watch it, laughing, as the world ends to the beat of horse's clopping.

In the introduction to my book *Dragon Daily News*, a collection of silly stories for children, I paraphrased Thoreau and wrote: "In silliness is the preservation of the world." The world presses down on us with relentless reality, often unfolding in ways that seem to make no sense. How could such things happen in a sane world? we ask ourselves. But the world is not sane. It can be as crazy beautiful as the arms of a spiral galaxy or human eye. And it can be as crazy ugly as anencephaly in which a baby is born without parts of the brain and skull, or a flu virus that suddenly mutates and kills tens of thousands of people. Or all the not-so-nice and horrific things we do to each other daily. Sometimes, all that saves us is our ability to laugh.

Tears are overrated, if you ask me. Beware of anyone who cannot laugh. Run for the nearest exit. Nicanor Parra, a Chilean poet who died recently at age 103, frequently wrote poems marked by absurdity. Explaining his relationship to the reader, he said: "Humor makes contact easier. Remember that it's when you lose your sense of humor that you begin to reach for your pistol."

Whenever I get particularly depressed by the doings of my fellow human beings, I try to do something silly. It is a personal act of defiance against a world that seems to grow more absurd by the moment.

Maybe I'll wear a silly T-shirt or write a silly poem. I'll do like Shel Silverstein in his wonderful poem "Put Something In": "Do a loony-goony dance / 'Cross the kitchen floor / Put something silly in the world / That ain't been there before."

Though not always succeeding, I have tried to be an honest man. But far more important to me is to be a silly man!

GENE TWARONITE is a Tucson poet, essayist, and children's fiction writer. He is the author of nine books, including two juvenile fantasy novels as well as collections of essays, short stories, and poems, and a forthcoming picture book. His poetry book *Trash Picker on Mars* was the winner of the 2017 New Mexico-Arizona Book Award for Arizona poetry. Explore more of Gene's writing at his website: thetwaronitezone.com.

Absurd Life Press